PREFACE

■ ■

AT THE END OF THE last date I ever went on as a resident of New York City, the check came and I grabbed it. "I'll get the next one," she said.

"A next one would be nice," I said, "but I'm moving to L.A."

She was an actress but couldn't find a facial expression.

"What? Why are we even—? When?"

"Soon."

She pulled a nifty override of her central nervous system and said, "You'll do very well out there."

To this day, I wonder if she meant that as a compliment.

At the time, April 16, 1989, there was a gratifyingly seedy exhibitionism in saying "I'm moving to L.A." It was tempting to delay the move just to have more opportunities to say it, but no. May 30th at JFK airport felt like the end of an era. Now, twenty-three years later, it's pretty clear that every second of every day is the end of an era.

Odd thing... The actress was twenty-four. Whenever you date someone much younger, women friends ask, "What do you even talk about with her?" As if, on dates with women my age, we spend an hour on the Cuban Missile Crisis.

Odd thing... At a party in Venice, the very short, middle-aged host/producer, natty in a suit from the Armani boy's department, tore his Achilles tendon rising on his tiptoes to kiss the cheek of yet another twenty-four-year-old actress. L.A. is either the happiest or saddest place in the world. As if there's a difference.

Odd thing... Choosing what to bring to these parties is a plague. For a potluck Grammy party, I made eighty-five calls before buying a selection of pastries at porterhouse prices. Upon arriving at the party, the first visible object was a huge bucket of KFC.

Odd thing... One Grammy party guest worked at The Museum of Tolerance. I suggested an exhibit devoted to lactose. No reaction. Nothing.

Odd thing... a woman at Starbucks described someone as a Christ-like figure. I said, "You mean he had a beard and a really low percentage of body fat?" No reaction. Nothing. Must be too soon.

Odd thing... it just seems strange that God only had one kid.

Seven years of writing *Seinfeld* episodes turned a reasonably normal inner life into a generator of perpetual "odd thing" thoughts. It's an unexpected but not unpleasant way to live. Sometimes, looking back at the sheer luck involved in getting to this nice place is overwhelming. Through all the striving and angling of life, people blindly assume everything they do edges them closer to some blissful place they can't name or describe. Everywhere you look, they're rowing through the day in what they absolutely know is the right direction, even while seeing people just like them going so obviously all wrong. Humility gets on my nerves, but I do feel lucky to live this particular life in a country where everyone thinks that as long as you have a paddle, it's okay to be up shit creek.

Whatever. Some people collect bobble-heads; I collect thoughts. The big upside is feeling productive, or potentially productive, all the time. Writing is the job but so is basketball, lunching, calling the gas company, getting Graves disease, stopping at a light, being held up at gunpoint, napping and anything else that might trip an original thought. A day with an original thought is my IPO, FDA approval and Good Housekeeping Seal of tacit approval.

Since stepping back from TV, I shove my thoughts into old familiar places like magazines and op-ed pages. Granted, still striving to be in print puts me a little behind the curvature of the earth, but blogging feels like it's for people who can't get paid to write. Although I do blog when I finish a piece and realize it

MANDELA WAS LATE

Odd Things & Essays From the *Seinfeld*
Writer Who Coined *Yada, Yada* and
Made *Spongeworthy* a Compliment

BY PETER MEHLMAN

THE SAGER GROUP

Artifex Te Adiuva

MANDELA WAS LATE:
Odd things & essays from the *Seinfeld* writer who coined
yada, yada, and made *spongeworthy* a compliment.
By Peter Mehlman

Cover designed by: Siori Kitajima, SF AppWorks LLC.
Formatted by: Siori Kitajima and Ovidiu Vlad for SF AppWorks LLC.
www.sfappworks.com

Cataloging-in-Publication data for this book is available from the Library of Congress.
ISBN-10: 1481250779   ISBN-13: 978-1481250771
E-book published by The Sager Group at Smashwords.
info@TheSagerGroup.net   info@MikeSager.com

■ TABLE OF CONTENTS ■

doesn't quite work. In any case, all of it's a joy: even in my early years at *Seinfeld*, part of me already missed writing full sentences.

Not that *Seinfeld* wasn't endlessly joyful. It was unalloyed joy. It was like a second shot at college—aside from harder work for grotesquely overpaid wages and a two-month spring break. Otherwise, it was hanging out every day at the coolest frat house on campus with funny people and—in lieu of freshman girls—oppressively gorgeous actresses.

You know, with your eyes, your skin, your hair, your lips and your body, you and I could make a beautiful child together.

Odd thing... There's a lot you never get to say in real life. Then there's so much you wish you didn't say. You get to middle age and wonder if the median comment you've made in life is, "You can move the seat back if you want."

I guess hoping for some record of having said something worthwhile before you die is a good reason to write essays and articles. Which isn't to say that's my reason. So many writers say they write to see what they're thinking about. That always sounds (over the) borderline pretentious. Really, is it so superficial to write just because you enjoy it? Isn't it an endlessly good game to see little moments in the world and to try making some sense of them? Never playing that game is like spending your life singing "Ninety-Nine Bottles of Beer on the Wall."

On the other hand, a friend framed her divorce papers as proof of having taken part in whatever the hell it is we're all taking part in, and it gave her a nice boost.

Odd thing... When friends or acquaintances get divorced, I always ask them if they knew, walking down the aisle, the marriage wouldn't work. So far, more than 90 percent said yes, they knew it wouldn't work.

Odd thing... People make so many mistakes it's unbelievable.

In this collection is a piece called "Star Trekking" that appeared in the *New York Times Magazine*'s "About Men" column on October 16, 1988. At the time, I wrote freelance magazine stories, an accidental career choice after working for Howard Cosell at ABC Sports. Throughout my two and half years at ABC, Cosell periodically said to me, "So Peter, what are your plans?" The implication was that he would fire me very soon, and it was always good for a laugh. In an office at 7 W. 66th Street on December 15, 1984, Cosell said, "Peter, this is the most painful moment I've had at this show, but due to budget cuts, we have to lay you off." I smiled and said, "Wow Howard, you're really taking this joke to a new level." Howard Cosell didn't laugh.

The truth is, among hysterically funny bosses, Cosell edges out Jerry Seinfeld. It's nice having a funny boss.

Before ABC, I wrote sports for the *Washington Post*. No one was especially funny at the Post. That was my role because of the way I got the job: After hearing that the Post was not hiring white males, I wrote a job letter as a white woman and sent it to Managing Editor Howard Simons (played by Martin Balsam in *All The President's Men*). Seeing as there were no meaningful qualifications on my resume, the letter was all jokes. Purely based on the letter, I was offered a job by mail as a copy aide on the 7 p.m. to 3 a.m. shift with Mondays and Tuesdays off. It was a job worth jumping for but . . . they were expecting me to be a woman named Faith Michelle Kates. I wound up writing a second letter as myself, explaining the first letter and was promptly invited in to meet with Simons. I remember wearing a white boat neck sweater to the meeting and saying something about Mary Tyler Moore that made Simons laugh, but not much else.

A few months into being a copy aide, I accidentally hung up on a correspondent phoning in a story from India. Okay, I hung up on him twice. The point is I was so incompetent as a copy aide that, purely for damage control, the powers at the *Post* just let me write.

There may be one or two lessons to be learned from that story.

Less than two years after "Star Trekking" was published in the *Times*, I submitted it to Jerry Seinfeld. No one else running a show in Hollywood would even read an article as a writing sample, but he did, and gave me a shot to write a script. At the time, I'd hardly ever written dialogue beyond a spec script for *The Wonder Years*. When I got word that "The Apartment" was well received, I had a sense that, even though *Seinfeld* was barely on the radar yet, my life was about to change.

You'll do very well out there.

It got back to me that my story became an inspiration among freelance magazine writers in New York. Because of a magazine piece he wrote, he's now making a fortune writing for *Seinfeld*!

I did try to feel, actually feel, the enormity of such good luck, but beyond becoming a big fan of the randomness of the universe, I couldn't quite get there. In a totally unplanned life, *Seinfeld* was another great town I clunked into after another manageably sharp, blind left turn in my career. Old friends used say, "You haven't changed at all," and I'd think, "Tell me what to change into and I'll try it." After a few years on the show, I even made a conscious effort to go on an extended ego trip. It just seemed like forgetting the little people should be a natural and underrated entitlement from writing for such a critically acclaimed hit show.

Odd thing... If you have any shred of human decency, it's really hard to even identify the little people.

Although—although!—the morning after we shot "The Implant," starring Teri Hatcher, I felt so good about myself, I called an old girlfriend. She asked what I was up to. (She doesn't know?) I told her I was a writer on *Seinfeld*. She said, "That's my favorite show. I never miss it."

What she did miss was my name popping up on her screen every week. And it wasn't as if it was plugged in the middle of the credits for fourteen camera operators. No, it was there, alone, right after "And Jason Alexander as George."

So the ego trip never got much off the ground.

The truly palpable benefit of *Seinfeld* was writing stuff that could potentially occupy a tiny place on the cultural landscape of America. Writers naturally anticipate the world shaking a little whenever their work reaches the public, but it never does. Or hardly ever. So when you happen to think back on a lunch you had in 1987 with an editor who used the phrase "yada, yada" and write a script based in part on that one phrase, which causes the phrase to wind up in the *Oxford English Dictionary*, you really learn to appreciate the wonder of it all. Frankly, I thought the term "anti-dentite"—from that same episode—would be the one that would catch on. But fine, it was "yada, yada" and it was—is—you know, pleasing.

I used to say that working on anything after *Seinfeld* was like dating again after your wife died. Yeah, that was a little over-dramatic... and ultimately, not true. In fact, there was a smooth transition from, say, hearing an NPR story about the Today Sponge going out of business and immediately thinking how great it would be if Elaine loved the sponge and bought out all that were left on the Upper West Side. Or reading about Sammy Sosa's sudden jolt of home run hitting and wondering why no one suspects Philip Roth of doping after turning out brilliant novel and after brilliant novel well into his sixties. The latter, which wound up on the *New York Times* op-ed page ("Zuckerman Juiced"), practically "wrote itself" during a 15-minute shower. From reading the Sosa story to getting the acceptance from the *Times*, four hours elapsed.

It's hard to figure why instant gratification has a negative connotation.

Odd thing... You never hear of someone who just takes steroids recreationally.

Odd thing... Never mind the back-story, but at recent dinner, a person my age asked, "Who's John Updike?" The moment was so astonishing that now I'm not sure it really happened. So while you may be thinking this is a story about an idiot, I'm thinking it's a story about epistemology.

Fourteen years after *Seinfeld* ended, I still come up with *Seinfeld* story ideas at a pretty good clip. They just happen. I still write them down with notations like, "Jerry story; or George in a pinch." Knowing there's nowhere to put them is just an annoying detail. I mean, how great would it be if Kramer met Maya Lin at a party and somehow convinced her to redesign his bathroom?

You'll do very well out there.

Well, whatever she meant by that, I'm here. We wind up where we wind up and as much as people say it all happens for a reason, it doesn't. I'm glad for that: Randomness makes for bad religion but if you write for a living, it's your church. And what a church! Show up, don't show up, the God of Random really doesn't give a shit. But he does send down some interesting ideas for you to write about now and then. You say "Thanks." He says, "Hey, I'm

God." You say, "Yeah, keep telling yourself that." And boom, you have a religion.

Odd thing... One night while doodling during a Laker game, the play-by-play guy said, "Shaq is on a roll," which was shocking because I heard, "Shaq is on parole." A TiVo rewind put the world back in order but prompted a thought of how funny it would be to listen in on Shaquille O'Neal meeting his parole officer. During increasingly sociopathic doodling, other parolees came to mind, one after another. Finally the vision of a parole officer with Nelson Mandela landed. Two days later, *Esquire* accepted "Mandela Was Late."

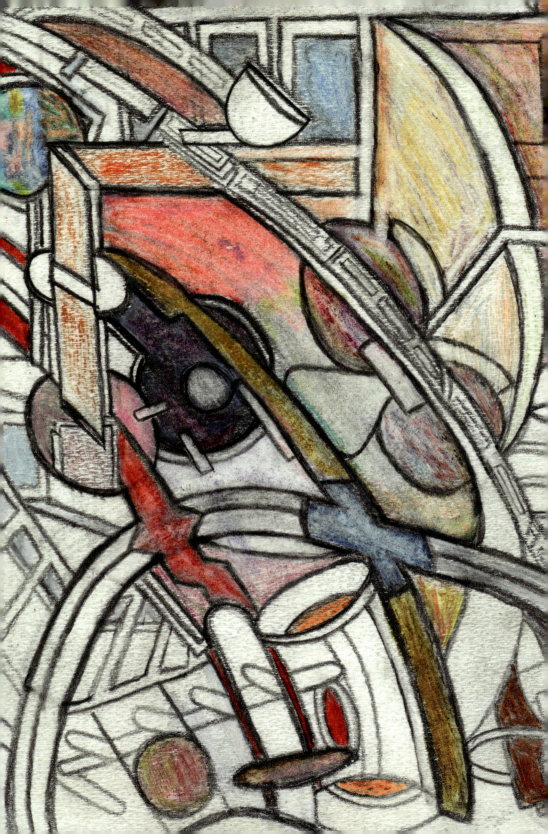

MOVING VIOLATIONS

■ ■

ONE NIGHT AT A DIVE on Franklin, the waitress was so beautiful that if she'd lived in any other city, they'd be naming a street after her. Instead she lived in—"Refill your coffee?"—Los Angeles. Gazing at her, I had a thought: *God, I really should consider moving out here.*

Then I had another thought: *I've been living here for six years.*

Without seasons or weather serving as speed bumps in time, your past goes on the lam at such breakneck speeds here, it's hard recalling when any events in your life occurred. That morning on State Beach walking Izzy when a dead body washed up—was that two years ago or five? June or November? Was *CSI* airing? Keeping track of time in L.A. calls for some sort of mnemonic device, some way to slice up the years. With a close friend and TV writing colleague, Marjorie Gross, we once contrived our own versions of L.A. seasons: Fire Season, Flood Season, Riot Season, and Pilot Season.

Not long before she died of cancer—June 7, 1996—Marjorie realized we had it all wrong: The fires, floods and riots didn't really happen to us. We may have smelled something burning or gotten a little damp, but if not for the media, we'd have lived happily in our overpaid bubble without knowing a thing. "To mark time, you need events that happened to *you* personally," she explained. She had a good point, and for years that point haunted me. Finding a recurring event that would bracket the eras of my past became a preoccupation, an inner scavenger hunt.

Then one day, I saw a squad car pulling someone over, the pretty lights playing against the canyon wall on the PCH. That's when it hit me: moving violations. In twenty-two years and roughly 350,000 miles of L.A. living, the moments of being pulled over by the police were the perfect connective tissue that defined my years in this town—just frequent enough, and traumatic enough, to reflect an evolving—and regressing—state of mind.

PULLED OVER NUMBER 6
Brrruupp!
The spotlight bleached the dashboard; the block-lettered voice—"Silver Audi. Pull over!"—blew through the vents. It felt good to be wanted. After eight years of no moving violations, I was back in the game. Turn signal, glide to the curb, weapon-free hands on the wheel. It all came back so easily. The cop was a young fireplug with muscles popping out all over Wilshire Boulevard. I'd just finished playing basketball at Crossroads School in a gym endowed by the celebrity parents of savagely over-privileged kids. The NBA-caliber floor left me so gamy with endorphins, I asked the cop's flashlight, "What's up?"

He performed that almost-smile designed after the '92 riots. A zillion dollars in property damage made police realize that if they lost law-abiding citizens in Audi A6s, this city was done for. Scanning my license, he asked,

"Where's Rustic Road?"

"Down 7th past San Vicente..."

"Do you know why I stopped you, sir?"

"To find out where Rustic Road is?"

Lacking cleavage to get out of tickets, I go with jokes. This cop laughed. A first.

"You were talking on your cell phone."

This was disappointing. During my panic attacks of 2001, I made all my calls in the car. If my dry spell was ending here, a sexier ticket would be nice. And to make things even more platonic, I was innocent.

"Officer, you're mistaken. My phone is in my sweats. If you want to see the call records..."

He took a second. "Maybe you scratched your head or something."

"Possibly. I just played basketball."

His face said, *What does that have to do with anything?* So I said, "I don't know what that has to do with anything."

He searched my pupils for signs of a recent visit to one of the pot shops in Venice. He glanced at the new hardcover book on the backseat: *Freedom*, by Jonathan Franzen.

"I'll take your word for it. Have a nice night."

PULLED OVER NUMBER 5

For the year after the terrorist attacks of 9/11, I pointedly made calls while driving. Focusing on the blah details of other lives distracted me from driving, an act that had launched countless, inexplicable panic attacks. A shrink was helping make the attacks explicable, but several months in, I started arriving late for sessions. The truth is, I didn't know what to discuss anymore. I'd run out of material. No way I could fill fifty minutes.

In a flimsy form of passive aggression, I'd stop at Starbucks before my sessions. One day an adorable barista wearing Planet Earth earrings said I'd look cool with a stud in my ear. I told her I didn't like intentionally puncturing my skin. Her thrilling laugh supplied a therapy topic for the day. Minutes later in my Audi I listened to my mother in Queens gleefully recount how she'd returned a sweater she'd bought on sale and got ten dollars more than it cost before the sale. "The dopey salesgirl didn't care," she told me. "It's not her money."

That sparked an idea: Record conversations with my mother and compile them as a much funnier version of the Shoah project. With my development deal at DreamWorks and access to Steven Spiel—

Oh, wait. I'm not sure that a not-for-profit oral history was part of the signing bonus.

Brrruupp!

"Are you getting pulled over?"

"No, Mom. But I have to go."

"License and registration, please."

"Wasn't I in the flow of traffic?"

"There were no other cars."

"Really? I'm going to my shrink, so it's not like I'm in a rush."

"Are you mentally ill?"

As yes-no questions go, that was a good one. When you have panic attacks, it's one you ask yourself. When I noticed that the cop resembled Lee Harvey Oswald, my heartbeat revved up.

"Do you need to call your doctor to tell him you'll be late?"

"It's a she, and she's just an MSW, not really a 'doctor.'"

"Do you—?"

"No. I try to be late because I have nothing to say anymore." Talking, even this idiotically, slowed my pulse just like the time a panic attack was instantly soothed by the words "911. What's your emergency?"

I got to therapy thirty minutes into the session. Please excuse Peter's lateness; he was doing fifty-two in a forty zone. The therapist eyed the Starbucks cup. "Did you get the coffee before or after the ticket?"

Back in the car my assistant, Chi, asked me over the phone, "Do you want me to take the traffic school test for you?"

"Uh, no. I'll just pay it. I probably won't get another ticket for years."

PULLED OVER NUMBER 4

The H in PCH gets people killed. Highway implies fast. Even if you've traveled the road a thousand times and know there are sneaky red lights and crosswalks coming up, those long straightaways make you race. When the sitcom you created has recently been canceled, names of network executives find twitchy nerves in your head that push your right foot.

Brrruupp!

"Where are you going, sir?"

Channeling *Get Smart*: "Would you believe . . . *Daytona*?"

The cop's face went clinically dead. Sorry, but such a punchy line—organic to the situation—deserved better. And don't kid yourself, I delivered it nicely. I've been around funny people. I know—

"Sir?"

"Oh, sorry. I had a thought about *Seinfeld*. See, I used to be a writer—"

"I *hated* the last episode."

While the officer checked on my fugitive status, Dream-Works called. ABC said they hoped I'd pitch them another show. A hippie who looked like he'd been preserved in formaldehyde slowed to gloat as he rolled past in his dented Volvo: "Maybe now you'll slow your pig car down when you drive through Malibu."

I told DreamWorks: "I wouldn't do another show at ABC if the future of Israel depended on it."

That line got around town. A pricey fine *and* a dinged reputation, all in one traffic stop.

As I drove away minutes later with my ticket, Chi called. When my DreamWorks deal began seven months before, it felt embarrassing to hire an assistant to take care of my tiny little life. But you get used to stuff.

"Do you want me to take the traffic school test for you?" she asked.

"That would be *so* great."

PULLED OVER NUMBER 3

After *Seinfeld* shoot nights, the writers and actors would meet at Jerry's Famous Deli in Studio City to review our biggest regrets about that evening's episode. It was such a can't miss ritual, that D, an actress on a lame show with whom I was having an intra–studio lot affair, understood when I told her that I wouldn't be home till late. One night over black-and-white cookies, Jerry said he preferred doing the show in L.A. because, with all the long hours, he'd feel like he was missing out on something fun if we shot in New York. Oddly, his attachment to New York made me realize that L.A. was my home.

In the deli's parking lot at around 2 a.m., my friend Marjorie, a fellow *Seinfeld* writer, said she wouldn't sleep because she had chemo the next morning, so it would be okay to call her as soon as I reached my place in Venice to report how long it took me to get back. I'd never beaten twenty-three minutes, and she couldn't grasp my failure. "It's not the sound barrier! What's so difficult about going a little faster?" I told her I'd try harder and call her the second I got home. Being friends with Margie at this time entailed a lot of reporting in. When it came to anything personal in my life, no matter how trivial, she needed to hear it first. Borrowed time isn't satisfied with secondhand news.

At the on-ramp to the 101, I glimpsed Kato Kaelin in the next car. Jerry had met Kato at a party months earlier and said, "So, Kato, what the hell happened that night?" It was a perfect Jerry line. But now, seeing this major witness in the trial of the century driving alone in the dead of night made me wonder how I could love L.A. so much while being sure it was the saddest place on Earth. Monster cranes lined the perpetually under-construction 405. Like luminol on blood, trillion-watt spotlights raised livid gashes in guardrails and black skid marks that swerved across lanes. Peace of mind in L.A. depends on sublimating the massacres that have taken place just below your feet not long ago.

On the West 90, flicking between rock stations in my '92 Saab convertible, I vetoed Don Henley's complaints about the city and settled on Talking Heads for the wide-open, 2.7-mile freeway—originally built for God-knows-what reason.

Brrruupp!

"Sorry, officer. I'm coming home from a *Seinfeld* taping. I'm a writer. And I got caught up in this song on the radio by . . . Bachman-Turner Overdrive."

Before profiling went mainstream, I profiled a cop. BTO is white-cop-with-mustache music, no?

"I have you speeding on radar."

"Do you ever catch anyone on sonar?"

He looked at me as if I were talking in pig latin. "You were going seventy."

My next words sort of slipped out. "SEVENTY???" That's the slowest anyone has ever driven on this road."

At home I called Marjorie and told her what had happened.

"I was worried. You need to get a car phone."

"Uh-uh. Never."

Around 3:15 I awoke to the sound of automatic weapon fire. D., the actress, screamed in her sleep, then jolted upright. The gunfire had undoubtedly come from a half mile away in the Oak-wood section of Venice, which for a time had one of the highest murder rates per square mile in America.

"Sound carries at night. The shooting was miles away," I lied.

"You need to move out of Venice."

"Uh-uh. Never."

Actually, Venice was a bit freaked by a post-riots rumor of a Crips initiation in which inductees drove at night with their lights off, waiting to shoot anyone who flashed their high beams at them. Welcome to our gang.

It was always gratifying entering the *Seinfeld* set with a morning anecdote. After a half hour of speeding ticket stories, a writers' assistant pulled me aside and said, "You know, we have a guy who runs a comedy traffic school. You won't have to sit in class all day. Just show up at the end, and he'll sign the form."

"Really? Fantastic!"

The writers' assistant pointed to a stand-in on Burt Reynolds's show *Evening Shade*. "That's our guy." I caught his eye and nodded discreetly.

"Speeding ticket?" he bellowed.

Walking by, Hal Holbrook wheeled around and sourly shook his head. Studio lots must have been quieter in his day.

My timing wasn't great. Previously "our guy" fixed traffic school in exchange for merely connecting with the cool kids on campus. No more. "If I do this, I want a part on Seinfeld . . . a speaking part."

Weeks later I arrived at a Hollywood hotel conference room at 5 p.m. sharp. A dozen or so violators, stoned on pure, uncut boredom, were lined up for traffic school certificates. The stand-in saw me waiting.

He did a capable job with his line in "The Sponge."

PULLED OVER NUMBER 2

Okay, this next episode wasn't technically a moving violation. But chapters in autobiographies are usually bracketed by some squiggly lines, so just go with it. For the most part I've deleted from my résumé the fact that my first TV job was writing an episode of *Wings*, an NBC sitcom created by three writers from *Cheers*. A few weeks in, I realized that I'd been writing lines for Steven Weber's character that should have been written for Tim Daly's and vice versa.

The morning after my realization, I hit Washington Boulevard in Venice for a to-go cup of coffee. I'd planned to try a place on Hill Street called Starbucks, but there was no time. The lines were so long, you'd have thought the coffee was laced with heroin. When I walked out of Joni's Coffee Roasters, a police car was blocking my '89 Sentra, which in my fog I'd somehow parked at an angle, the front wheels trespassing a parking spot directly outside the store entrance, the back wheels in the spot just left of that. A mountain of flesh in uniform stood over my trunk, his eyes locking in on me the closer I got to my car. After sensing my ignorance/innocence, he explained that armed robbers park diagonally for quick getaways. He'd blocked my car "to prevent a potential high-speed chase."

"Sorry. I wasn't thinking. I have to get to work early. I'm a writer on a TV show." Then, a first stab at coolness by association: "It was created by *Cheers* writers. It's called *Wings*."

"Never heard of it."

"Yeah, neither had I before I got the job."

"Look, go to work. But if you ever do this again, your ass is mine," he said.

"Thank you." Then: "Those high-speed chases—they must get pretty hairy."

With a smile that could chill Norway: "Sometimes they're fun."

On the *Wings* set, my armed robbery story sparked one response: "Is your script done?"

A week later I had a second date with a neighbor. Upon hearing "*Wings* fired me," her face scrunched up. She eventually moved back to Denver.

PULLED OVER NUMBER 1

As a freelance magazine writer in New York, I avoided personality profiles. But after moving to L.A., I needed money and took on all comers. Profiles for *Us* magazine were my cash machine: Billy Baldwin, Jennifer Jason Leigh, Patti LuPone, Arsenio Hall—all people of interest in the summer of 1989.

Nevertheless I rented a sluggish AMC on floating credit. My rent in Venice was double that of the studio I'd recently left behind on East 63rd Street. Even with the bazillion celebrities in L.A., my monthly nut was looking like a tough cover.

Then I turned left from Del Rey Avenue onto Washington Boulevard.

Brrruupp!

I reached into my glove compartment for the rental agreement.

"Freeze! Hands on the wheel!"

That's how I learned that people in L.A. carry guns.

Back at the Venice Canals, an actress from Denver told me about comedy traffic school. It sounded like a good story for *GQ*'s comedy issue. The illegal left netted a $1,250 profit. It was almost worth it. The traffic school comic had one recurring punch line: "... next thing you know, you wake up dead."

During a break, another detainee said that if you worked on a Steven Bochco show, they had a guy who fixed traffic school. You just had to show up at the end of the day. I shook my head and said, "That's despicable."

BLANK

■ ■

EUGENE BRUSCA HAD NO OPINIONS on anything. Each day at his home in Santa Monica, California, he read an array of archliberal and staunch conservative editorials, then vice versa. Yet, at the end of each column, he inevitably concluded, "Wow, that's something."

For years, Brusca assumed he was not an opinionated person simply because all the really good opinions were taken. But when he found himself unable to come down pro or con on the subject of famine, he sought professional help. Saline Flax, a world-famous lab technician, performed an MRI and CAT scan and diagnosed Brusca with rare form of ambivalence. Alarmed, Brusca sought a second opinion, but no doctor would see him without a first opinion.

Eugene Brusca was at wit's end.

This was no time to be an American without a stash of fully loaded opinions. The nation was more divided than ever, with some predicting it may soon be subdivided and turned into townhouses—another issue on which Brusca had no opinion.

Living in Santa Monica only made matters worse. With its myriad voter propositions and swarms of leggy socialists, this city was as a known hotbed of activism where having no opinions on the great issues of the day was considered idiotic. Hence, Brusca's effort to conceal his condition became a full-time job, although he could often work from home.

For years, Brusca assumed the local citizenry suspected something about him was slightly off, but they were quite tolerant. When they'd ask his opinion on a topical issue and his vital organs would completely shut down, they'd usually give him the weekend to think about it. They graciously invited him to politically lively cocktail parties, during which Brusca desperately tried to steer conversation away from politics and back to cocktails. For this, he was widely admired in the fashionable seaside community as "a good listener" and "a pill."

On the rare occasions he did try to contribute to political debate, the results were disastrous: When a neighbor opined that the war in Iraq cost too much money considering that some people right here in America could barely put food on the table, Brusca suggested that perhaps these people simply didn't have the proper utensils. When another neighbor suggested that stem cell research could cure multiple sclerosis, Brusca said, "One sclerosis is bad enough, but multiple..." After both these comments, he was met with an unnerving silence, and only through deft usage of the words "just kidding" was he allowed to have dessert.

If that was a narrow escape, it barely compared to the recent national election when his cover was nearly blown altogether. Usually, after carefully reviewing the policies of rival candidates, Brusca would vote for whoever was taller. No American can forget the presidential election when the heights of the candidates were left off the ballot, but this omission was especially devastating for Brusca. After he cast a write-in vote for Kareem Abdul-Jabbar, heavily armed agents from The League of Women Voters raided his home and told him to cut it out.

Such close calls occurred regularly for Brusca since, between primaries, run-offs and propositions, Californians vote every Tuesday. His stress level grew steadily until finally he pondered a move back to his native Detroit where, throughout his childhood, he was ignored by people of all races and creeds. Such an uprooting of his life would be a rash undertaking considering he'd just vacuumed, but frankly, he preferred the even more extreme measure of turning back the clock to a time when a good clump of the world lived under communist dictatorship. A land where one is not "entitled to his opinion," would have suited Brusca well. A land where one is entitled to his opinion but is shot for saying it aloud would have also been good. In fact, while watching the fall of the Berlin Wall in 1989, Brusca said, "Gee, I kind of liked communism. You know, except for the money part..."

(In retrospect, this was the most forceful opinion he'd ever voiced. Unfortunately, the acoustics in Berlin were poor at the time, and the Germans only responded by saying, "Not now, I'm hammering.")

While Brusca agonized over his decision, he stopped attending all local functions. He officially became a hermit by filling out some forms and renaming his home "The Hermitage." Then one day while Brusca was lounging on the fence in his backyard, there was a knock on his door. Brusca tried to pretend he didn't hear the knock, but he wasn't that creative, so he just went ahead and opened it. Standing there was a man from the Gallup poll. He wanted to ask Brusca if he had any opinions on anything. Caught off guard, Brusca said, "No," to which the pollster said, "Thank you for your time," and went away.

Holy cow, thought Brusca, *I blurted out my secret and... nothing. Have I been looking at my situation all wrong Is it possible that ignorance is a valid point of view?*

Emboldened, Brusca knocked on his neighbor's door. Mickey Fowler was a hyperopinionated, left-wing billionaire who once described Mao as a "capitalist pig." Fowler came to the door wearing a cumbersome metal brace on his knee, and Brusca, sensing a good icebreaker, said, "What's with your leg?" Embarrassed, Fowler said, "I fell down the stairs of my Learjet and tore my ACLU." He invited Brusca in for a drink then off-handedly said, "You know, Brusca, we're destroying the planet." Brusca replied, "Well, we'll have to make do without it."

Fowler's eyes narrowed, then widened, then went back to their normal size. "You have no opinions, do you, Brusca?"

Brusca nodded in the affirmative. "No," he said.

"Stay here a sec," Fowler said. "I'm going to make a call."

Fowler pulled out his credit card, picked up the phone and bought the *Los Angeles Times.* As his first order of business, he gave Brusca a job as a columnist. Every Wednesday and Sunday on the op-ed page, fourteen column inches of utterly blank space appeared under the byline of Eugene Brusca, for which he won the Pulitzer Prize. The Times increased his column to four days a week with no visible decline in quality. With his readership soaring, Brusca became a fixture on the lecture circuit. At each lucrative speaking engagement, he would take the stage and say absolutely nothing. Following would be a brief question-and-answer period, in which rapt audiences never asked any questions, then stood for prolonged ovations. When local, national or international crises erupted, Brusca became a sought-after panelist for town hall meetings at which his repeated refrain, "Beats me," never failed to send audiences home feeling more at ease with a tumultuous world. In short, Eugene Brusca was fast becoming a household name. Even at places of business, some people knew his name. The Times increased his column to six days a week and sold its sponsorship rights to the Travel Bureau of Finland. Finally, after nearly two years, Brusca started to feel his completely vacant column was getting stale. His editors encouraged him with such classic journalistic phrases as, "Come on, Eugene," and "Don't be silly, Eugene." But it was all to no avail.

Brusca took a leave of absence to recharge his batteries, but somehow he never got around to it. For a while, his editors called him every day hoping he'd regain his inspiration. Soon their calls decreased to once a week, then back up to three times a week before diminishing to the occasional greeting card. Wars broke out, natural disasters ravaged cities, scandals rocked Wall Street, politicians sucked the marrow out of the state, poor people suffered, rich people slept late and Eugene Brusca gradually faded back into obscurity. Though sometimes he hung out in his den.

So, Then They Gave Out the Emmy for Sitcom Writing and, Well, Yada, Yada, Yada...

■ ■

THE CURIOUS THING ABOUT NOT winning an Emmy is that you get better gifts than you get for winning. It reminds me of when I was in college and my aunt sent me ten dollars for my birthday. Two months later, when I got mononucleosis, she sent me fifty dollars.

Anyhow, I don't want to create any false impressions: I'm deeply sickened about losing. So much so, I envision friends at my memorial service saying: "He was never the same after losing that Emmy."

The source of all this wasted emotion began March 5 when *Seinfeld* finished shooting episode No. 0819: "The Yada, Yada." It was our 145th episode, but when director Andy Ackerman said, "It's a wrap," a wave of young love euphoria warmed the set, a euphoria we felt after such episodes as "The Contest" ("master of my domain") or "The Outing" ("...not that there's anything wrong with it").

I co-wrote the "The Yada, Yada" with Jill Franklyn, a friend who's not on staff but writes beautifully oversexed screenplays. I turned to her and said, "Get out your Emmy dress."

Zipping forward to April 30, after months of anticipation, Ellen DeGeneres came out of the closet as a lesbian during a one-hour episode of her sitcom, *Ellen*. That particular show was titled,

"The Puppy Episode." I missed it because I was reading a book, but Jill said, "If we get nominated for an Emmy, 'The Puppy Episode' will be our main competition."

"No, " I insisted, " 'The Puppy Episode' is an hour. We're in the *half*-hour comedy category."

"You think so?"

"Sure. An hour comedy is a completely different form of writing."

July 24, 1997: Apparently not.

The hourlong "Puppy Episode" is nominated for an Emmy in the half-hour comedy category, along with three episodes of *Larry Sanders* episodes and "The Yada, Yada."

I am more relieved than anything. None of my scripts has ever been nominated before. Not "The Sponge" ("spongeworthy"), not "The Implant" ("double dipping"), not "The Hamptons" ("shrinkage"), not "The Smelly Car." ...The rest of my resume is available upon request.

Anyhow, I really want this nomination, and now I have it.

And it seems so right. "Yada, yada" is sweeping the nation. President Bill Clinton uses in a speech. Katie Couric says it on *Today*. "Yada, yada" is even added to the new *Webster's Dictionary*.

Unfortunately, I already know I'm going to lose.

Even as a competitor I can see it clearly. "The Puppy Episode" has the kind of emotional moments Emmy voters like to reward. A week ago, I overheard a woman at my health club saying that she cried during "The Puppy Episode." And as everyone knows, if you make people cry, you can win an Emmy for ... comedy writing.

At *Seinfeld*, poignancy is forbidden. And really, if you think about it, 95 percent of the world is on the verge of tears anyway, so it's no big trick to push them over.

I whine about "The Puppy Episode" being an hour (only to learn, eventually, that there isn't a separate category for longer episodes). I whine about about how lesbianism isn't exactly big news ("It's 1997!"). Then I am assured by an actress friend that "The Puppy Episode" meant "the world" to her lesbian friends.

So I try to change my mindset. I start thinking how the eight weeks between the nominations and the awards will be a great time in my life. It goes sort of like, *Okay, I know I'm going to lose, but there's a ray of hope that I'm wrong.*

The thing is, you can live pretty well on a ray of hope.

July 25: I stop off at the *Seinfeld* office. I should mention that I'm no longer with *Seinfeld*. After six years with the show, I joined DreamWorks to create my own sitcom.

Jeff Schaffer, one of the writer-producers, tells me I'm going to win the Emmy. And that seals it. Now I know have *no* chance. Zero. I love Jeff Schaffer, but his powers of prediction are so off he can barely see into the past.

August 5: The writer's arm of the Television Academy hosts a party honoring the writing nominees. Since I know I won't be honored on Emmy night, I'll take anything I can get. *Politically Incorrect* nominee Arianna Huffington tells me I'm going to win the Emmy. We become friends.

August 10: I come up with the first line of my acceptance speech: "You know, I didn't want to just win this Emmy. I wanted to win by a lot."

August 23: I happen to know this is the day the Emmy voting takes place. I wear the exact same clothing as I did the day I was nominated. Unfortunately, on Emmy day, I have to wear black tie. Five years ago, when *Seinfeld* was racking up nominations left and right, I went haywire and bought an Armani tux. After a spate of Emmy Awards, Golden Globe Awards, People's Choice Awards, and Writers Guild Awards, this ceremony will bring down the amortized price of my tux to just under $400 per wearing.

September 1: My DreamWorks office is on the same lot in Studio City as *Seinfeld*. I bump into Jerry and tell him, "I really want to win. It's not enough just to be nominated."

"Of course not," he says, "it's a slap in the face."

Another opening line for my acceptance speech pops up. Before the audience stops applauding: "Okay, okay. You can stop applauding. It's not like this is a Nobel . . . it's just an Emmy."

Weird. Even for an award you're willing to denigrate, you still want to win it more than you've ever wanted anything in this whole wide world.

September 2: I chat with Julia Louis-Dreyfuss at the *Seinfeld* craft services table. I tell her how much I want to win and she says, "Of course. If you didn't, you'd be an idiot."

Julia won last year and is nominated again. I ask her if she cares much this time around. "Not really," she says.

Not caring. That's the place where I want be. In fact, that's where I usually am. But not now. I care. I care way too much.

September 12: At a Writers Guild party honoring the Emmy nominees, I bump into a friend named Dava Savel, one of the writers of "The Puppy Episode." We chat amicably, wish each other luck and mingle with others.

An elderly woman sees my name tag, touches my hand and says, "You're going to win."

I take her at her word and start feeling like, maybe . . .

I go to the bar to get a drink and there's Dava talking to Richard Frank, president of the Television Academy. Mr Emmy. As I reach them, I hear Mr. Emmy say to Dava, "You're going to win."

Dava sees me and, embarrassed, says to him, "Don't say that. Peter's one of the other nominees!"

We chat amicably. Meanwhile my mind races: *Does Mr. Emmy know something? And if so, would he really tell Dava ahead of time?*

My guess is no to both questions, but I investigate anyway, sidling up to Mr. Emmy and asking, "So, out of curiosity, how many people on Earth right now know the Emmy results?"

Only too happy to respond, he says there are just a few and they all work for the accounting firm tabulating the votes. He then describes the security process in such exquisite detail, I realize he was just predicting that "The Puppy Episode" would win . . . not unlike how I was predicting "The Puppy Episode" would win.

I'm relieved. Now, I can maintain my false hope for another two days.

September 13: I play golf with an Emmy voter in my category. He says, "I voted for you but I have to say, there was a lot of *Ellen* sentiment in that room."

September 14: There's not much to say about the actual Emmy night.

My limo driver went fifteen miles in the wrong direction before making a U-turn toward the Pasadena Civic Auditorium, where I realized I forgot my Emmy tickets.

Without even showing ID, got a replacement set for Row T where I sat down next to my date, Jill, and her date, and Martha Stewart, who read a book and ate a plum as "The Yada, Yada" lost early in the evening to *Ellen* in front of a worldwide TV audience of 600 million people

It left me slumped in my seat for the next two and a half hours, looking like a commercial for strychnine.

On top of that, *Frasier* won for best sitcom. When talking to a reporter after the awards, I have a thought that I almost have to throttle myself to NOT say: "I don't get it: *Ellen* wins for coming out of the closet and *Frasier* wins for never coming out of the closet." Again, I did not say that. Politically incorrect sour grapes are the kind of stuff that gets you deported out of the entertainment industry, back to America.

Epilogue: It's amazing how you can have such low expectations and still be so disappointed. I guess it has something to do with how a moment that should be so suspenseful can turn out so predictable.

Or, maybe in a quiet way, I'm just very in touch with my own superficiality and wanted, for one night, to revel in it.

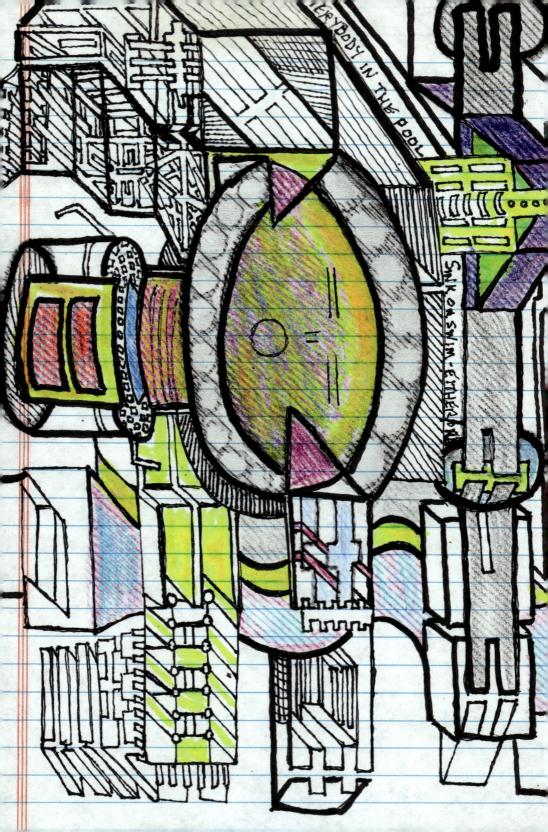

EVERYBODY IN THE POOL

SINK OR SWIM · EITHER OR

DEAR GUILTY MOGUL, COUGH UP

■ ■

IN SANTA MONICA CANYON, WHERE mailboxes are dressed
in peace signs and "Impeach Bush" stickers, and letters come
stamped with guilt. Of Monday's eight envelopes, four carry "USA
NONPROFIT ORG." postage: A.S.P.C.A., National Disaster Search
Dog Foundation, Project Angel Food and something from Paul
Newman. (Can't I just send him some old receipts for the popcorn
and the marinara?)

There are metered letters from the Brady Campaign and the
Southern Poverty Law Center, along with a stamped invitation
to a fundraiser given by a classically trained alcoholic; a please-
come-home letter from James Carville seeks to lure Democrats
back into the money-wasting business after we checked out in December 2000.

On the walk back from the mailbox, I think of John Updike
ending his memoir by saying you should appreciate the walk back
from the mailbox. No one appreciates that walk like sitcom writers. When *Seinfeld* residuals first filled my mailbox, I cherished
that walk. But now, having to choose between guns and search
dogs drains me with donation fatigue. Maybe Mr. Updike makes
only story editor money and doesn't get hit up much, but my walk
from the mailbox has become a daily replay of *Sophie's Choice*.

All right, maybe I'm over-dramatizing. But I am tired. Los
Angeles may be the ripest solicitation target in the history of the
world. Fundraising preys on guilt, and guilt is part of our routine

living expenses. So many Hollywood people are so grossly over-paid and liberal that charity is the only way to head off schizophrenia. On top of that, show business does much of the overpaying, and in recent years the industry's crushing pettiness has risen to a new low. Like a mafioso steadfastly going to church on Sundays, the deputy network head of prime-time comedy development can feel vaguely human by writing a check to help the Children of Chernobyl.

Even outside the office, Los Angeles has turned mean and angry. It used to be enough to see the guy tailgating you nailed by the police two miles up the road. Now you want to see him and his Escalade wrapped around a tree with its 345-horsepower Vortec engine and Nokia 3200 polyphonic-ring cell phone splattered in a freeway triage. (Wait. I can't believe I thought that. I've got to give to Meals on Wheels.)

Deciding which of the daily spray of plea letters gets a donation reminds me of dealing with the homeless in New York during the 1980s. For baseless reasons, one poor soul got a dollar, another a quarter, the third a mumbled "no." Fundraisers know what they're doing. Their letters are as hard to look away from as the hollow, pleading eyes of the homeless.

I charge a donation to the A.S.P.C.A. The address labels they offer are really nice.

On Tuesday, nine solicitation letters. Combined, the minimum suggested contributions total $1,245. Three are from familiar names: Jerry Lewis, Jimmy Carter and Robert Redford.

Mr. Redford is something of a god in this town, for which he seems to have nothing but contempt. He's smart, innovative, committed and still pretty strong at the box office. When he gets behind a cause, Hollywood sits up. "Redford," people say in the hushed tones usually reserved for people like Nelson Mandela. "He really walks the walk."

I saw Mr. Redford at a Knicks game when I was 13, so when his name is on an envelope I usually pony up.

If you happen to befriend big Hollywood stars, directors and moguls, their causes really grab you when they marry. They sense that having one of the world's largest private collections of money makes it a little dicey to register at Macy's, so: "In lieu of gifts, please send a donation to the Something of Something for a Free Tibet."

When the divorce rolls around, the ex-spouse suddenly favors a repressed Tibet and hits you up for that. There are remarriages and new causes, and your plea mail multiplies like paramecia.

Then again it's not just maximum wage earners who embrace causes in Los Angeles. Charity also flies when careers thunk. Suddenly uncastable-unbankable-uninsurable quasi-stars take time out from their empty schedules to go headlong into the abolition of, repeal of, cure of, preservation of... everything. Their enthusiasm bubbles: "Saving snail darters is so rewarding that I can't believe I cared so much about all the show business drivel you still care so much about."

When these people ask for donations, it's somehow easier to decline.

Wednesday brings the Invasion of the Environmentalists. The Natural Resources Defense Council, the Nature Conservancy, the Sierra Club, Heal the Bay. One that grabs me immediately is Bat Conservation International. It is a great organization. Bats are misunderstood creatures: fascinating, gentle, doting parents and prodigious pollinators of the desert Southwest, they are under constant siege from farmers who don't realize that bats consume tons of flying pests in one night. You really ought to give.

It's odd how so many ex-New Yorkers who grew up untouched by nature (does Central Park count as real nature?) are rabid environmentalists now that they live in Los Angeles. For many, it took having children for them to notice that the world is on its last legs. The Natural Resources Defense Council, with its high-powered lawyers and ferocious vigilance, seems to be the favored organization. Besides, it really knows how to get you.

Some of its mail comes addressed directly from Robert F. Kennedy Jr. It regularly updates its impressive victories and dire warnings about the next catastrophe—all with a stamped return envelope that just dares you to steam it off and glue it onto your DirecTV bill.

Stamp or no stamp, environmental organizations live in a world of the worst-case-scenario; some days you can't take it. You just take their word for it and write a check so that you can delude yourself into thinking the blue marlin will make a comeback.

Your check spawns endless calendars in the mail, every month dotted with photos of exotic animals frolicking around the endangered species list. Lions, whales and toucans stare from your walls, thanking you for your generous support and asking for more.

Along with Thursday's four letters from usual suspects—Emily's List, Children's Hospital Los Angeles, Firefighters Charitable Foundation and the World Wildlife Fund (spectacular calendars)—there's a letter from George Allen, the conservative Republican senator from Virginia. What does he want from me?

Nothing. The letter found the wrong mailbox. The couple next door are such wonderful neighbors that I almost forgot that the husband is one of the rare Republicans in the area. As if my own mail doesn't wear me out enough, here's an all-new moral problem: whether to toss Senator Allen deep in the recycle bin for the good of mankind. Wait a minute. I can't do that. I'm part of the solution, not part of the problem, right? I'm not sure. The right wing thinks it's part of the solution, too. We can't all be part of the solution, or there would be no problem.

They are great neighbors. They came to my birthday party, and our dogs are best friends. I put the letter in their box, hoping my neighbor feels the same way about the Republicans that I do about the Democrats. In 2000, I gave a hefty check to the Democratic Party in an effort to help it win back the majority in the House of Representatives. As a reward, I got fifteen minutes of quality time with Richard Gephardt in the lobby of the Peninsula Beverly Hills. I liked his politics and wanted to talk policy.

He wanted to talk *Seinfeld*.

A month later, Gephardt called me in my office. Not an aide. Mr. Gephardt himself. He talked about how important another donation would be. Then, sounding as if he had taken a Berlitz course in Los Angeles-ese he said, "Ten would be great" (ten thousand dollars, that is). In the ensuing weeks, months and years, I was tickled to know I had reached a point in life when I could regularly duck calls from the former minority leader of the House.

Dear Guilty Mogul, Cough Up

Now I enjoy blithely recycling nine or ten letters a month from the Democrats. Still, you have to feel for politicians. They have no choice but to constantly beg for money without the luxury of being sure it's really for a good cause.

Friday: AIDS, Democrats, diabetes, sheriffs, ozone, art, children, hunger and whales. Topping them off, the American Civil Liberties Union invites me to join so I can be assured of living in a nation where I'm free to contemplate my own guilt.

Of course the sheriffs get a check. When the Los Angeles police ask for a donation, you say, "How high?" Diabetes. Didn't I give to them recently? Yes, I did. Hey, this is a thank-you note!— along with another solicitation. Okay, all charities do that. And it's better than the ones that ask you to renew your support when you never gave in the first place. Still, can't they just thank you? Can't they just acknowledge that you're a giving person, someone who cares, someone who's off the hook for a year? No. You're never off the hook. They have reeled you in, you're flapping around the deck and they throw another wormed hook at your mouth.

On Saturday, a residual check for the 18th rerun of a "Seinfeld" episode I wrote nine years ago.

Before I moved to Los Angeles from a below-street-level studio on the lower Upper East Side of Manhattan, I used to joke about my do-goodism by telling people I was an appendix donor.

In scattered moments, I miss those days.

Stop Go Stop Go Sto

EXT. MICKEY FOWLER'S HOME - MOMENTS LATER

Eugene... on a deck. Mickey ... a ...

EUGENE
What happened to your knee?

MICKEY
Oh, I tore my ACLU.

Eugene reacts. Mickey looks at the ocean and s...

MICKEY
You know, Brusca, we're destroying
the planet.

EUGENE
Well, we'll just have to make do
without ...

NARRATOR
At this, Mickey's eyes na...
then w...ed, then wen... b...
their no...al st...

MICKEY
...do you support gay mar...

EUGENE
...ly for ...os...u...

...
You ...ave ... or ...in... do you,
Brus...

EUGENE
N.. I do n...

MICKEY
Hold on, I'm go... make a ...
...Calls on ...ad... phone...
Hello, ... I ... ... the number for
the P... ... es... Times...
...es, I ... ... ke to buy ... L.A. Times.
(Pa...) ... it's not a ... roduction. I ...
w... ... ly th... icle paper ...
b... ... erical express...

to B = forever ... more than that
A to Z = more than that

Any slower?

JUMP ...

...inat...... ...04.09. ... Thank you.

NUMEROLOGY

■ ■

IN 1967, FOOTBALL JERSEYS WERE a teen fad in New York City high schools. The world was decades away from maniacal sports marketing, so the jerseys were bloodless: no team logo, no team colors, no superstar stranger's name along the upper back. Just white jerseys, striped shoulders and a sullen, boxy number. The fad seemed radiantly dull… until a trend emerged. The number. The number was the same on every jersey.

I was preteen and groping: Sixty-nine. Why sixty-nine? Why *sixty*-nine? Why *sixty-nine*?

My father had season tickets to the New York Giants so I was up on the NFL. Number sixty-nine on the Giants was Willie Young, a left tackle notable for standing over a crumpled quarterback freshly mauled by the right defensive end—Young's responsibility. During one game, in our bleacher seats at Yankee Stadium, a virtuoso drunk sitting behind us shouted, "Young, you're a fat shit." Shriveled in embarrassment at hearing such filth in the presence of my father, I nevertheless sensed the fad could not be centered on a fat shit.

Sixty-nine felt like it had nothing to do with football at all.

Confirmation came on a busy day at Davis Delicatessen on 188th Street and 73rd Avenue in Queens where some older kids cackled from hearing a counterman shout, "Sixty-nine? Number sixty-nine?" Consciously oblivious adults fingered their cash or glared down at the smoked white fish, hoping they'd jump out

of their walleyed deaths and bite one of the snickering, prema-
ture ejaculators on the ass. If anything other than sex led kids to
laugh and parents to play dumb, I wasn't aware of it. Then, as now,
I was incapable of stopping my thoughts from drifting to undesir-
able places. I started thinking that sixty-nine could possibly mean
something really debauched.

At eleven years old, all mysteries were dark mysteries and
all dark mysteries involved sex.

Actually, let me back off on that a bit. The summer of 1967,
had been called "The Summer of Love." What activities, exactly,
comprised a "summer of love" were lost on me. It sounded groovy,
maybe even out of sight, but it was no dark mystery: I was unaware
of any connection between love and sex, so I couldn't be bothered.

The cases that consumed me were breathier: A "psychedel-
ic shop" called Bell, Book and Candle opened on Horace Harding
Boulevard, just around the corner from where, a few months earlier, kids threw snowballs at Mayor John V. Lindsay in protest of
the city's slow cleanup after a blizzard. While looking at strobe
lights, I heard one of the oppressively relevant deejays on WNEW,
the legendary progressive rock station, talk about this song by the
Doors called "Light My Fire." "It's great sex music," he said. "It has
the long version for regular sex and the short version for a quickie.
On these airwaves, we only play the long version."

Quickie. Now there was an intriguing term. I looked it up in
a dictionary. KWIK-e: A book or movie produced in very little time.

You know who didn't get much pussy? Noah Webster. But
at the time, if it didn't make the dictionary, it couldn't be too
important.

Another fascination came in October when my classmate,
Eddie Clark, peered down and to his right during glee club and
whispered, "Gail Morrisey has a great ass."

That one had me confounded for two solid days: A great
ass? Is that something I'm supposed to be looking at? Ultimately, I finessed my way around that one too: Okay, I'll look at asses,
I'll talk about asses, I'll compliment asses. I can do that. After all,
there they were, lined up in alphabetical order every day for all the
world to assess.

But sixty-nine was different. It couldn't be so easily dismissed. The number was the fad, and it had to mean something specific and crucial to life in the cheeriest country on Earth.

Seeing as this was a sexual investigation, I ditched the *Dragnet* procedure of starting my search close to home then expanding outward. It wasn't like I could canvass my own household. I assumed recreational sex was new, something invented around 1965 and my father—working on 23rd Street in Manhattan—and my mother—at the office of PS 179—were too absorbed in making America great to possibly be up on the latest in fornicational chic. I used to look at them and their friends wondering how it was possible they'd all had sex. Now I look at my friends the same way. What comes around is even more appalling when it goes around.

Although I should mention that my parents, after a Broadway show, did take us one time to dinner at Max's Kansas City, the hottest New York restaurant among the burgeoning hippie scene. *Oooo, look out you rock n rollers... here come the Mehlmans.* All the crazy long hair and off-smelling smoke was scary and thrilling, as was the girl who smiled at our out-of-place nuclear family then flashed us the peace sign. Her braless breasts, if used properly, could have inspired the Vietcong into an unconditional surrender. My father flashed the peace sign back.

Maybe my parents *would* know what sixty-nine means...

No. I was a subversively conventional child, a studious angel who couldn't be known to explore weapons-grade vulgarity. Confidential sources would have to be cultivated outside the home.

I carefully considered possible educators. The choices were dodgy:

The first was Kenny Kantrowitz. Despite doing his second tour of fifth grade, Kenny had an impressive grasp of all matters taboo. He didn't let his fixer-upper of a brain keep him from staying in touch with the ex-peers who had zoomed past him into sixth grade right on schedule. Sixth graders at PS 26 knew stuff.

The plan was to sidle up to Kenny and mention that on a math test I'd gotten a grade of sixty-nine, then hope he'd break into his Jurassic laugh and explain everything. On a Friday morning, I went up to Kenny in the auditorium as he labored over something he could just about identify as "a book." He seemed grateful for the interruption, so I launched Part One of my plan. But when Kenny more or less congratulated me on my math score, I nodded and walked off toward the front of the auditorium. My friend Anthony Milano asked me what I talked to Kenny about. Math, I said. He gave me this faraway look, which was understandable as it had only been a few weeks since Anthony had convinced Kenny that Mount Rushmore was natural rock formation.

My second source was Gary Lauer, a perfect combination of older, friendly and pitiful. Because of his huge nose, Gary's nickname was "Face the Nation"—so dubbed by his best friend Mike Bostick. (Mike had flair in this area. His black cat was named "Willie McCovey.") Considering the constant abuse Gary took for his prematurely grotesque profile, I hoped he'd be flattered anyone would seek him out for anything. I caught up with him as he watched pickup basketball in the schoolyard.

Gary never played sports, he just watched—as if he were a season ticket holder to his friends' lives. On this day, three of the ten players were wearing sixty-nine jerseys. Perfect.

"Little Mehl, what's up?" Gary said pleasantly.

I opened with basketball talk, noting that Phil Schoenhaut couldn't dribble to his left. Gary said, "No, he has no left hand. He has a right hand and non–right hand." I laughed. Gary had the kind of lively sense of humor I'd associated with aesthetically tragic people. I reasoned that there had to be some special dispensation from God to make up for the tyranny of chromosomes.

Pleased by my laughs, Gary made more jokes. I laughed more. Fun. We were having fun. So I threw it out there: "Boy, what's the big deal about sixty-nine?"

Gary's nervous system high-jumped, his face going all gargoyle, as if he were seeing himself in the mirror for the first time. "What did you ask me?"

I back-peddled. "The shirts, with the numbers. Oh, forget it..."

Too late. Face The Nation bolted up and waded into the middle of a fast break—that's how much this couldn't wait. He grabbed Phil Schoenhaut and whispered to him with Cold War urgency. Phil's braces, which required only slightly less wiring than the Triboro Bridge, pitched forward. I noticed that he went to his right even to wave over other players who, one by one, buckled in viral laughs.

I blew out of a side exit of the schoolyard. I ran home, just ran full-tilt, my head baggy with questions bigger than me. Tearing through a path between two buildings—the exact spot where Steven Swirsky told me President Kennedy had been shot—I bumped into Teddy Scharf. Teddy was six months younger than me, and yet he was wearing a sixty-nine jersey.

"Where did you get that shirt?" I asked, all Perry Mason.

Teddy got nervous. Real nervous. "It's my brother's," he said. "I grabbed it out of his drawer. I thought, you know, everyone's wearing sixty-nine shirts. I don't even know why. I just looked up sixty-nine in the Giants Yearbook. It's Willie Young and he stinks. I don't get it. Does sixty-nine mean something?"

So, Teddy was also on the case.

His research was a week behind mine, but I decided we could partner up. I brought him up to speed then warned him against questioning older kids of or even telling anyone we'd had this discussion. He nodded like a newly deputized narc. We went silent for a few moments, contemplating the world over our heads.

On an ensuing weekend, I walked home after hanging out at Eddie Clark's house, where he continued talking about Gail Morrissey's ass as if it were something hanging in the Guggenheim. I had almost a dollar in my pocket, so I decided to stop at Lorenzo's, a pizzeria next door to a bowling alley known as "The Hole." I was feeling cool around The Hole as I'd recently bowled my high game there with a ball so light the pins practically had to be bribed into falling. The sixteen lanes were downstairs from a nondescript doorway on Union Turnpike and the street outside the two establishments became a hang-out for older kids. I got two slices and a Coke and—

Two guys walked into Lorenzo's just as one said, "Believe me, I think he's full of it, too, but he swore up and down that he sixty-nined her in Cunningham Park."

Boy, information really rides on random currents. You just gotta stay open for business. I grabbed my pizza and Coke, ate on the move and ran to Teddy Sharf's house.

"I just learned something really big,"

"What?" Teddy whispered. "What?"

I paused to let the moment gain weight, then said:

"Sixty-nine... is a verb."

Teddy's eyes widened as if to say, "Holy crap." This was confirmed seconds later when he said, "Holy crap." I nodded. Yeah, holy crap. We stood there processing. It was getting cold. And windy. And in eight months, Bobby Kennedy would be dead and America would be in Chapter 11 for the rest of my life and damn it—

Teddy looked up at me and said, "You're shivering." I thought he was going to ask me into his house, but instead, Teddy, in his six-months-late-on-everything hopelessness, said, "Well, I still don't know what the hell sixty-nine is all about, but I'll tell you this much: When 1969 rolls around, all hell's gonna break loose."

BIG WORDS SMALL MIND

ANXIETY IS FUNNY, PANIC IS HARD

■ ■

IT SHOULD BE NOTED THAT the following account of a sudden on-slaught of panic attacks should be told in the first person, but he can't face up. After all, this Galaxy is outside his self-image. He'd always been so calm, his heart rate normally sixty beats per minute, his blood pressure that of a Syracuse sophomore on a trust fund. So how could this happen? How could he suddenly be sure he was going to pass out at any moment? How could he be too scared to drive on a freeway? How could he need to carry his phone around in his home so he could call 911 at a second's notice? How could he feel compelled to sit on his hands in his girl-friend's car so he wouldn't suddenly wrench the wheel from her as she drove down the Santa Monica Freeway on a rainy night? After years of basketball and grossly overpaid comedy writing, how is it possible that his days now swarm with shrinks and masseuses and acupuncturists and even the chiropractors at whom he'd tak-en so many prime-time potshots over the years?

You're wrong. It all started well before September 11. You're right, it may stem from gallons of repressed rage, but let's review his case anyway.

It began at the end of a trip to the University of Maryland last year, where, because of his sterling career in America's lowest art form, he was lauded as an outstanding alumnus. ("Forget teachers and doctors—let's honor the guy who makes white people laugh.")

Driving on I-66 to Dulles Airport for an 8:00 a.m. flight back to Los Angeles, he suddenly felt light-headed, before being over-run by a sense that he would swallow his tongue. He strangled the rented steering wheel. The two miles to the next exit was his Apollo 13, a slow-lane chance to contemplate dying. At a big build-ing on Route 123 in Virginia, he stopped and told a security guard he was in trouble. The guard took him at his word and called an ambulance. An EMT tested his pulse ("fine") and blood pressure ("normal") and asked if he felt like throwing up. No, he said, add-ing that he was riding a sixteen-year vomitless streak.

Emergency-room blood tests showed he was slightly dehy-drated. He received IV fluids, told Hertz where to find its car and shakily got a cab to Dulles. With a headwind and a chatty Sri Lank-an seatmate, the flight to Los Angeles took just under a thousand hours. But upon landing, he simmered: You had a bad day.

Two days later, he was driving to his health club when, ap-proaching the 405 freeway, his head swam again. He took sur-face streets to the gym, gripped the heart monitor of a treadmill and, without taking a step, rang up 120 beats a minute. Focused like sixteen-year-old gymnast, he drove home in the rain with the windows open and tried being rational: *You won't pass out. So what can happen? Perhaps a seizure. You've never had a seizure. Why now?* Then a term found it's way into his head: *Panic attack.* He felt at home.

The next morning, NPR reported that the space shuttle couldn't land because of high winds in Florida. All those brave but (they must be very) exhausted Americans able to look down and see Florida (what? maybe ten times a day) yet unable to get there. Panic attack. 5:00 a.m. Then the shuttle couldn't land the next day either. He screamed in bed: "Find an unwindy airport some-where and just end it already, dammit!"

Freeway driving became his biggest anxiety producer. When he'd tell show business associates over the phone that he didn't really drive on freeways anymore, the line would go silent a mo-ment. Then, assuming their ears had been duped by some fiber-optic glitch, they'd simply move on, telling him about a meeting in Burbank. (The 10 to the 405 to the 101 to the 134. Exit Pass Avenue.)

His doctor ordered tests: an MRI of his neck ("perfect"), an ultrasound of his carotid arteries ("gorgeous"), a CAT scan of his coronary arteries ("immaculate").

This clean bill of health depressed him no end. He so wanted a physical cause for his emotional wreckage. Earnestly, his doctor asked if he used cocaine, heroin, Ecstasy, or crystal meth. When he laughed and said he was the only person in his college graduating class to have never taken a Quaalude, he got a prescription for Xanax.

Half a .25-milligram pill (a minuscule dose) worked nicely. Never having gotten drunk in his life (a root cause of all this?), he now grasped the phrase "takes the edge off." And if the edge stayed on, he took another quarter of a pill. For example, if he was meeting his girlfriend three miles away but outside his driving axis— he'd take three quarters of a pill. (Well, for the ten-minute drive, he'd also leave a full hour ahead of time. And before that, he'd do a series of yoga-like exercises. And to forget he was driving, he'd listen to a tape of himself being interviewed on the NPR show *Fresh Air*: self-absorption to keep him from being self-absorbed.)

Like anyone else having panic attacks, he began seeing a therapist. Unlike anyone else, he chose his therapist for her location. He and his five-minute-drive of a therapist delved into why all this was happening. During the first session, she said, "Okay, so you won't drive on the freeway. So what?" Wow. That was an eye-opener. He got permission to give himself a break. How about that? They moved on to the repressed anger thing and how, after seven thrilling years as a *Seinfeld* writer and then two more producing his own show (*It's like, you know* . . . canceled so that *Who Wants To Be A Millionaire* could have another night), he was now in the second year of a lull. The next pilot he wrote, one he loved more than life itself, didn't sell. Rejection. He couldn't believe it could happen to him. Then the theories got more personal. Even before the Maryland trip, people were dying all around him. Fathers of best friends; forty-six-year-old friends of friends dropping dead at father-son doubles tennis matches; total strangers collapsing two feet away from him on the street in Santa Monica—the ambulance arriving, sirens blaring, to drive the poor soul off in a final blaze of glory. That string of death and funerals capped by pastors and rabbis making a living by doing their pathetic stand-up acts without knowing shit about the cross-armed, pine-boxed star of the show—

Oops, he thought, there's the rage again. But bigger than that was a simple fear of dying. And what's wrong with that as a cause for panic attacks? It made so much sense: driving was the most readily available method of being killed, and that's where the attacks were most pervasive.

His therapist said that panic attacks often hit men in the forties. Huh. He'd seen loads of them lurch in or out of iffy marriages or forsake sex for consumer electronics or suddenly wear baseball caps backward. But panic? Apparently.

After canvassing his soon-to-be-ignored demographic, he saw that panic seemed rampant, as did tips on what to take ("A tiny, tiny dose of psychotic seizure medication") and whom to see. One person recommended a Christian Science nurse, which seemed to him way too easy a job.

He was told the attacks wane on their own, and, in fact, within a month, his emotions made a bumpy landing on a tolerably heightened plateau. Panic yielded to intermittent, (mostly) manageable anxiety. Now, when seeing an elderly man sprinkle three packets of Equal on some scrambled eggs at Jerry's Deli, he could talk himself out of a repulsed meltdown.

He spent most of his days monitoring himself moment to moment. He became his full-time job, a labor of self-love. Because he could sleep, eat and work, a lonely voice of sanity in his head calmed him when, for example, he'd (illegally) walk his dog on the beach but stay a safe distance from the water in case he passed out. (*You've never passed out. What if I do now? The ocean would wake you up. Yeah, then it would pull me under. Oh, look, a dolphin.*) The voice was even on duty for dinners with friends, where he no longer said outrageous things to jumpstart crippled conversations.

After a few months of this uneasy peace, another panic attack bombed through his roof at 2:00 a.m. on a Sunday night. This attack was so wanton, he called 911. Just talking to a dispatcher cut his heart rate in half. He got up, looked through his sweaters, got dressed, ambled down to his living room and blithely flipped through the *New York Times Week in Review*. He laughed at something in Maureen Dowd's column. When the ambulance arrived without wailing it's embarrassing siren through his hushed canyon, he became almost serene. At 2:45 a.m., watching the Pacific Coast Highway recede out the back window on his way to St. John's Hospital, he had philosophical thoughts: *You have to take the bad with the bad. Or, maybe I can get a sitcom out of this.*

That's when he gave in and started seeing the psychopharmacologist. After the doctor concluded that his new patient wasn't clinically depressed, just suffering from panic disorder, he prescribed Zoloft with a twist of Klonopin. The Klonopin (kind of like Xanax but with a longer half-life and less of a rebound effect) would keep him from having panic attacks on a daily basis, while the Zoloft took its own sweet time—more than a month—to really settle everything down.

Unfortunately, the 2:00 a.m. panic left him unable to be in his home alone for fear of another attack. ("Anticipatory anxiety," the psychiatrist called it. "It's textbook.") For a week, his godsent assistant had to stay at his house. Then his brother gallantly flew out from New York.

One night, talking on the phone with a friend, he mentioned that his assistant was on her way to stay over. Casually, his friend said, "Why? Are you afraid you're going to damage yourself?"

He hung up and felt his heart go back into overdrive. He hadn't thought of suicide but became instantly fixated on it. First he felt compelled to throttle himself. Then he became acutely aware of his wrists and the inside of his elbows—any convenience store of veins. He threw out every sharp knife in his house and felt better. No great loss. He never cooked anyway.

His psychiatrist reassured him that he wasn't suicidal. It was just a "textbook impulse." Each time his symptoms were called "textbook," he felt euphoric. Just an average, garden-variety neurotic: That's what he was aspiring to.

It's nice at this point to mention that throughout his entire bout with panic, people kept telling him how great he looked.

Whether they knew what he was going through or not, people everywhere would see him and say, "You know, you really look great. What have you been up to?" One of those people was the insanely talented and wise actress/director/writer Mary Kay Place, who, upon hearing of the panic attacks, said to him, "For what we do, panic attacks are just a rite of passage." This bit of kindness reassured him for upward of two hours, a new record at the time.

When the dose of Zoloft slowly climbed to 100 milligrams, he eased back into himself. He spent his first night alone in six weeks. He got back on the freeway, going one more exit every day until he made the drive to his office and back.

Now he drives the freeways every day—but with bizarre caution. He stays close to the road shoulder. He barely speeds. He uses turn signals. He avoids road rage at all costs and plays tricks on himself to get his mind off the fact that he's driving. (He now considers his car phone a vital safety feature.) One day, he had an epiphany about the whole driving phobia: Maybe this is how people wind up moving back to New York.

Then September 11 happened. Heart sick about the tragedy, he also felt a certain guilt-racked comfort in knowing that New York had caught up to his level of panic. Not that he was weighing a move. After all, there are now more and more days in L.A. when he's totally fine, when he functions like a full-time player in whatever this game is. Yet he can't quite see the day when he floats above his consciousness again, when dying seems as far off as it used to. So he's trying to give himself a break. When his mind trespasses to how he's a different person than he was a year ago, he takes a breath and manages to forgive himself the shame at having an ailment that's all in my head.

AN L.A. STORY

■ ■

AROUND HERE, YOU GOTTA LOVE what you drive.

No wait. That's the slogan for Mercedes and not at all what I meant to say. I meant to say, around here, you gotta have a story with a satisfying beginning, middle and end, but the truth is, there are 4 million stories in Los Angeles and lots of them don't amount to anything.

So, I lost my credit card.

After watching a baseball game at a pub on Fairfax with an actor friend whose character was being written out of the TV show *Studio 60*, I tried cheering him up by pouncing on our check, only to find my MasterCard missing. Right away, I knew where I lost the card.

That afternoon I had gone to the Kinko's at Wilshire and Sixth in Santa Monica to copy a news story about a man who shot four strangers. Turned out he was mentally ill. Somewhere between START and JOB COMPLETE, I flashed back to the latest colossally pretentious commercial I'd seen for KCRW. I'm sticking with KPCC, I thought to myself while grabbing the copies... and forgetting to retrieve the MasterCard.

So I gave the waitress my American Express card. The difference between cards escapes me, but I use MasterCard to roll up the frequent flier miles that I give away to East Coast friends so they can come out here and disrupt my life for a week. The Amex is purely for wallet aesthetics. Sure enough, it had expired.

Right away, I knew why I had an expired card. I'd been sent a new card, but I'm a little fast about tossing my mail in the recycle bin, even though I don't believe for a second that the L.A. Bureau of Sanitation reincarnates junk mail into legal pads for Manatt, Phelps.

The exasperated waitress was just a vocabulary word shy of calling me malfeasant, so I hauled out a huge load of cash. I have a Tiffany money clip too pompous to grip less than eighteen folded bills, so I constantly milk Wells Fargo to keep the clip satisfied. A few years ago, in lieu of the usual business gift basket, I got a gift certificate for Tiffany, a store so bulging with impractical items that all I could find was a silver money clip adorned with Roman numerals, the significance of which DaVinci couldn't decipher.

The waitress took the cash, saw the money clip and said, "Wow, bling, bling." When white people say "bling" or "street cred" or "holla," you know the words are officially extinct, but I shrugged, drove home and, immediately after forgetting to cancel my MasterCard, went to sleep.

The next night I went to the Dodgers-Mets game with a friend who coincidentally would be directing the first friend's last appearance on *Studio 60*. His euphoria over scoring the tickets was dampened by the disappointing early ratings of *Studio 60*. So to cheer him up, I assured him the show would catch on, even though I was a person who never saw the show and didn't have a valid credit card.

I picked him up an hour before game time at the New Otani Hotel in downtown L.A. According to MapQuest, the ride to Dodger Stadium would cover 2.11 miles and take six minutes. MapQuest ignores things like UCLA football games in Pasadena, USC football games at the Coliseum and music festivals downtown, so the six minutes was wildly optimistic. We ended up listening to the first five innings on the car radio. Around here, you gotta love what you drive in neutral.

Let me tell you something: The magnificence of Vin Scully describing a baseball game wears a little when you get gridlocked out of witnessing seven runners cross home plate.

We finally got to the turnstile, and my friend hurriedly produced the tickets, which weren't tickets but printed e-mails with bar codes. A scan of the bar codes indicated that the tickets were already being used by someone else now sitting in our box on the first-base line eating our Dodger dogs.

We walked to customer service, whose motto is "Sorry, there's nothing we can do."

"But I got the tickets through my agent!" my friend pleaded.

"Sorry, there's nothing we can do." Apparently, the customer service rep had gotten her job without the benefit of representation.

We walked to the centerfield bleachers, where I noticed fans leaving the stadium to smoke. A guard would initial their tickets so they could inhale and go back to their seats. We glanced at the initials on someone's ticket, wrote the same initials on our tickets and breezed into Dodger Stadium

Hello, is this the hotline number for Homeland Security?

In a way, I'd like to tell you that we went to our box, ejected the impostors and sat down just as the Dodgers staged a heroic ninth-inning rally. But we watched from the bleachers as the Mets celebrated on the Dodgers' home field.

A day later, I canceled my credit card and asked if there were any wayward charges. In a way, I'd like to tell you that a fortune in baseball souvenirs had been charged by someone illegally sitting behind first base at Dodger Stadium. But there were no charges, and not having a credit card for the next week didn't affect my life at all.

My friend's agent sent a gift in penance for the ticket snafu. In a way, I'd like to tell you it was a Tiffany gift certificate, but it was a gift certificate for a lobster dinner. I finally watched an episode of *Studio 60*, and while it had a nice beginning, middle and end, I figured it might not catch on anyway.

STAR TREKKING

LET ME ASSURE YOU, THE Saturday I spent walking around Manhattan trying to spot a celebrity, any celebrity, broke all the rules. Sure, my friends and I have hyper-evolved eyes for spotting famous people on the street, but it's not supposed to be a conscious activity.

During our regular male bonding sessions, Jake, Greenie or I might say, "Had a good spot today... Grace Paley on Bleecker." Or, sotto voce, "Eyes left... there's Pacino." But that's as excitable as it gets among thirty-year-old men too blasé to answer phones before three rings.

That's why that Saturday was so bizarre. Everyone I knew was out buying wedding gifts or pricing co-ops. Karen and I had broken up a month earlier after two years, due to irreconcilable similarities, so I wasn't very well grounded in planning solo days. She was at the Yale School of Management, where I'd been spending weekends watching her study quantitative analysis. It was more romantic than it sounds.

Now, lacking my usual stamina for sleeping, I woke up at 8, read the sports pages, ate and Dustbusted my studio into sterility. At 10, I lamely decided to go shopping. Spend therapy.

As I walked up East 63rd Street, I thought I spotted Tom Jarriel of ABC News coming toward me. But up close, I saw that it wasn't Jarriel. This flagrant mis-spot scorched me. My celebrity radar dish is hardly ever off target. Which is why at 63rd Street and Lexington

Avenue, I thought, I'm going to keep walking until I make a spot. It may take ten minutes or ten hours, but who cares? And wherever I am when I make the spot, I'll turn around, go home, order in a movie rental and call it a day.

Even with my eye, this was a cracked idea, but I was married to it. Shopping's such a trite therapy, and who knows, I reasoned, maybe I'll make one of the all-time great spots.

To date, Greenie's all-time best was the night we walked in the East 70s discussing the films of writer-director Robert Benton. Just as I said, "Benton is as good a writer as he is a director," who walks by with his dog? Right. Robert Benton.

My favorite occurred the day I was in midtown carrying a copy of *The Anatomy Lesson* by Philip Roth when boom! There's Roth walking right toward me. Usually, it's considered bad form to disturb a spotted celebrity in any way, but I was so excited by Roth's presence, I blurted out, "Philip! Zuckerman just got to Chicago! The book is brilliant!"

He gave me an oppressively literate smile and kept walking.

At 11 a.m. that Saturday, I entered Central Park at 72nd Street where I'd once spotted Claus von Bulow. I scanned a sea of anonymous sunbathers. So much exposure on all the wrong kind. Somehow this reminded me of the day when Jake said to me, "Isn't it comforting how celebrities tend to look worse in person?"

I said, "Yes, but the depressing thing is that you and I are only seen in person."

I headed toward Central Park West, and devised three rules for the day. Spots at Columbus—the Upper West Side restaurant—don't count (too much of a celebrity hangout). Nor do spots near the TV networks (too easy), nor spots related to *The Morton Downey Jr. Show* (a personal bias).

The first two rules guaranteed my mission's integrity: the spot would be a chance encounter with the one underlying feature of all chance encounters in New York: the probability that you'll never see the person again as long as you live.

I walked to 77th Street and Amsterdam Avenue where Karen and I once spotted Rusty Staub and Isaac Bashevis Singer within seconds of each other. Karen, who loves Singer and never heard of

Staub, was nonplussed by my excitement over the spots and said, 'You used to work for Howard Cosell... How can you still be so star struck?"

It's true, I did work on Cosell's show *SportsBeat* for three years, but as I explained to Karen, that experience only fueled my fascination for famous people. Being with Cosell and feeling the awe of onlookers was like fame by association. Of course, it was also a lot like the phantom limb syndrome: all sensations of fame without having it.

Those sensations made me see New York as the ultimate unattainable woman. Getting her to notice you at all is next to impossible. You can have green spiked hair and fifty million dollars stapled to your coat, but New York still tosses you into its pot of anonymity. The effort just to survive in this town would assure you cult status anywhere else. But here, only fame turns the city's head.

Karen didn't buy it. She was twenty-four then and still got more of a thrill bumping into old dorm acquaintances than from, say, spotting Scavullo. But by the time you're thirty, the more people you know in this town, the more people you'd pay not to have to bump into.

At 2 p.m., discouraged by the lack of notables, I walked to upper Broadway where I once saw Woody Allen. Citizenship in New York demands that if you see Woody, leave him alone. Don't say hello. Don't nod your head. And don't tell him you prefer his earlier films.

I'd have met these conditions, but Woody didn't show.

Back on Amsterdam, I stopped into Barney Greengrass "The Sturgeon King," an eatery with occasional spot potential: Dustin, Bianca, Calvin, blah, blah, blah... all lox eaters. All somewhere else today.

I ate a beautiful piece of fish and left. Crossing 86th Street, I turned to see who was getting out of a limousine in front of Barney Greengrass when a jeep ran the light, nearly bouncing me off a fender. There's no right-on-red law here, but straight on red is fine. Life in this city is like a constant struggle to die of natural causes. Then again, limos are now the transport of choice for accountants and associate producers, so I had no business turning around in the first place.

At 3:30, gravity started fiercely leeching onto my legs. I broke into rhythmic yawning around 57th Street and Seventh Avenue where, at assorted times, I'd spotted Nastassja Kinski, Daryl Hannah and Merv Griffin. Today? Tourists photographing the Russian Tea Room.

My whole day was starting to taste pathetic. There's enough weight on your psyche, I told myself, it's time to compromise: go home upon making a spot... or at five o'clock. Whichever comes first.

Within ten minutes, I flirted with another compromise: just hail a cab now and go home. It's no big deal. Lots of people in New York sell out their ideals. Of course, if Tom Wolfe got out of a cab right then, I'd be emotionally freed up for a more significant sell-out in the future.

Tom Wolfe? At that point, I'd have settled for Barry Slotnick.

I went down Sixth Avenue past ABC, a place that, since being laid off, always makes me queasy. Granted, the network is no longer the corporate waste playground it was when I was there, but some New York landmarks can beat down your best rationalizations. I fled the area.

At 42nd Street, I let a thought pull the rug out from under my whole day: when it comes to things like peace, love, happiness and celebrities, searching isn't always the best way of finding. Nice. A senseless day contrived into some vague perspective.

I turned toward home, walking slower and slower.

Laboring to Park Avenue, I envisioned Karen at the Yale library, plotting some widget firm's next move. More deceleration.

Two blocks up, a couple was window-shopping in slow motion. In fact, everything seemed to be going in slow motion: the traffic, the time, my feet, the way the couple turned around and the way I froze. The man with his wife... I couldn't believe it. Edwin Newman. Just when I needed him most.

I didn't care that he'd made a few appearances on *The Hollywood Squares*.

I got home at 5:10.

DODGING POTHOLES ALONG MEMORY LANE

■ ■

ON TRIPS BACK TO NEW York, I visit a street sign outside my old apartment on East 63rd Street near First Avenue. "Unnecessary Noise Prohibited." It's my sign, my permanent (whatever that means) contribution (whatever that means) to the city.

Ex–New Yorkers invest lots of emotion in inanimate objects, so I never feel overly demented staring at a sign no one else notices. I once met a man who on business trips to the city makes a detour to a hydrant near Carl Schurz Park, a spot where a dancer once said she couldn't live without him. He lives in Santa Fe now, and last he heard, she's in commodities.

When you live in New York, it's hard enough claiming any chunk of the city as your own, but when you're part of the diaspora, you are really lost. You're among (it must be) thousands of people walking around who once lived here but for some reason— love, ambition, allergies—moved. And now, on your couple of trips back per year, you're in this nether demographic. Not quite tourist, not quite resident. Your experience as a New Yorker, adjusted for inflation, has a street value of nothing.

I bolted eighteen years ago, and when I come back for a visit, the city is full of strangers who act as if the good old days are just beginning. Every time I come to town and take one of my strolls down repressed memory lane, my old landmarks not only offer little sense memory of my life in New York, they make me feel more detached.

Still, I try to fit in: opting for a hotel on a neighborhoody street on upper Broadway (the room edges out my old apartment for square footage), taking subways (embarrassingly slow with a MetroCard), except when I don't (barking out unsure routes to cab drivers). The big thrill is being mistaken for a resident by tourists asking directions.

"Do you know where there's a restaurant called Al Dente?"

"No idea."

I shrug and walk off. Al Dente. As if there's a restaurant in Rome called Undercooked.

The sad thing is, the inhabitants of the diaspora are even lower on the totem pole than tourists. At least tourists are wooed and/or accommodated and/or targeted. But no one invests in ex–New Yorkers. No one tries to make you feel as if you still belong. No one opens a restaurant aimed at people who lived in town during the '80s: A pasta-loaded joint with a smoking section, menus printed on junk bonds, waitresses in leg-warmers and photos of Bernhard Goetz on the wall.

No one runs a tour bus showing you around your old life:

"This is where your office was when you worked at ABC Sports. It's now the headquarters of the *Financial Times*. And ABC Sports is now folded into ESPN, and your boss died 13 years ago."

"This soon-to-be-new wing of Sloan-Kettering is on the site of the movie theater where you and your ex-girlfriend, who also happens to live in Los Angeles now with her husband and three kids, saw *Hannah and Her Sisters* twice on the day it opened, Feb. 7, 1986.""This is where you found a $20 bill as you got out of the subway just before having breakfast at Windows on the World."

No, you're left to your own jangled memories. I walk around New York so full of retrospect, I feel as if I'm looking back on things that never happened.

The truly weird thing is, I invariably wind up spending a day with another ex–New Yorker who happens to be in town, someone I probably had lunch with a week earlier in Santa Monica. There is an ease in knocking around with someone in the same fogged-in boat. We can safely laugh at how out of it we are while grasping at personal histories.

* * *

On a trip last month, I met up with a friend (who lives one ZIP code over from me in Los Angeles) outside Time & Life ("You know, Sixth and 50-whatever"). As it was summer, we didn't even have the benefit of looking more tanned and healthy than everyone else.

Walking east toward Madison Avenue, I flipped back to 1983 and recounted walking past the Hotel Elysée not two minutes after hearing that Tennessee Williams just died there. My friend remembered that day as if it were—well, maybe the day before yesterday: "Are you sure it was the Elysée and not the Warwick?"

I was sure. He wasn't. It became such a point of ex–New Yorker pride, we considered going to the Elysée to ask. Surely so notable a death would be a big selling point. But instead of making a potentially touristy inquiry, we retreated back to our Hollywood selves, guessing that, if Williams were alive and living in L.A., Paramount would have him writing *Suddenly Last Samurai*.

We laughed about it the way New Yorkers do. During lunch, I almost mentioned to him how, on return flights, when the pilot says we'll be landing at LAX in twenty minutes, I always smile. Another trip back to New York. Over.

And about that street sign. When I lived in New York, my apartment was on the ground floor, and the honking cars piling into the city from the Queensboro Bridge and converging into other cars trying to get out of the city made so much noise that friends would ask me why I was calling them from a phone booth. So in 1988, I wrote a letter of complaint to the mayor.

In the fall of 1989, I got a letter saying that the city would be putting up a sign on my street to discourage honking. The letter was forwarded to my new address in Venice, California, from my post office on 70th Street. That post office is still there, but my old ZIP code has changed.

OKAY, I CONFESS. I FINAGLED MY WAY OUT OF JURY DUTY

■ ■

LET'S SAY THREE MOMENTS PER week an average American concludes that, in this life, you just can't win. I'll follow up on that later.

Recently, I was Juror No. 6 in an Inglewood courtroom. Late into a third day of jury selection, the prosecutor, whose questions had been crisp and pointed, suddenly went off script, asking, "Does anyone feel they cannot judge the facts fairly?"

My hand disobeyed my brain and flinched—then backed down like an umpire deciding the pitch wasn't really a strike.

"Juror No. 6?"

Caught. "You know ... " I began.

Wait. I'll follow up on that, too.

This is the story of how fast the justice system mutated people who wanted to hear the facts, deliver a verdict and make America great into citizens hell bent on shirking our duty.

I love trials. While living in New York, I attended the "yuppie murder" and "Central Park jogger" trials. For the "subway vigilante" trial, I brought a date.

Maybe I was spoiled by sexy trials, but on Day One in Inglewood, I wasn't the only one of forty-two prospective jurors who drooped at the news that we were up for a misdemeanor case. Okay, it was two misdemeanors. And yeah, yeah ... one involved a gun.

The judge welcomed us, explained stuff a poodle would know, then dumbed it down: Five minutes on "no cell phones." Stolen glances in the jury box said: "You're the judge. Say no cell phones and end it."

We also heard a surefire way to dodge jury duty: Renounce your American citizenship. In all, the judge's one-hour monologue featured seven laugh lines prompting one rogue "Heh." Then he told us to come back tomorrow.

And oh, the trial should last between six and eight days.

How hard can it be to get a French passport?

On Day Two, we jurors didn't get into the courtroom until 2:10 p.m. When we heard that two people had been excused for hardship reasons, you could almost hear the rest of us glumly calculating how our odds of being chosen inched up from 29 percent to 30 percent. The idealism of Day One fluttered.

The judge began the *voir dire*. "Juror No. 6?"

I responded with name, occupation, jury experience and "Yes, in 2007, my home was burglarized, and my mother was carjacked at gunpoint." Pause. "Otherwise, I had a pretty good year."

The whole courtroom laughed. The defendant flashed me a smile.

At 3:20 p.m., the judge said that if he gave us a bathroom break, it would be late by the time we all finished. So he excused us for the day.

Outside the courtroom, a juror said, "After an hour we need to go to the bathroom? Are we children?"

Another juror whispered to me, "You made a big mistake in there."

"Really?"

"See, your mom was the victim of a gun crime, so the prosecutor liked you. But your joke about it exposed your humanity, so the defendant also liked you. You're screwed. We think you'll definitely be picked."

Apparently, many jurors who started off with good attitudes had boned up on the finer nuances of ducking jury selection. It was like they'd been spun back to 1969, reduced to kids trying to dodge Vietnam. Because of budget cuts, courts are closed the third Wednesday of every month. Because of heavy caseloads, Thursday was no good either.

When we returned on Friday, the prosecutor and defense attorneys got to question jurors and eliminate anyone they pleased

75

Okay, I Confess. I Finagled My Way Out of Jury Duty

with no explanation. Only there was no defense attorney. The defendant represented herself. When the judge gave her instructions, she'd respond, "Gotcha." Patience in the jury box trickled down around empty.

When questioned, some jurors gently told her she was foolish to represent herself, others less gently. She bounced chastisers with a cheerful "Juror No. 10, you're free to go."

During breaks, the remaining jurors stood around saying things like, "Juror No. 4 played it so smart! The second she cursed, you knew she was free. Why didn't I think of that?"

The pool was soon cut in half. From a hallway window, I could see my car on the garage roof. Would going on the lam be a misdemeanor or . . . ?

We all liked the young prosecutor. When the defendant asked if any of us had lost a child, the prosecutor calmly said, "Objection. Relevance."

As a *Law & Order* fan, I smiled at the familiar courtroom lingo. The defendant somehow saw me smile and smiled back.

Right then, I began rescheduling the next two weeks of my life. The word "sequestered" pockmarked my thoughts. But wait . . .

Remember when I said that the prosecutor suddenly went off script and my right hand rebelled?

"You know," I began, the creepy self-righteousness of a soapbox rising in me, "three of our state's biggest problems are deficits, crowded prisons and backed-up courts. Well, this case is a microcosm of all three. All this time and money wasted on a misdemeanor case. It's all incredibly frustrating."

Moments later, the defendant scanned the jury box deciding whom to set free. I locked my baleful eyes on her. Remember the theory of three moments a week making you think you just can't win?

I fled the court holding a little diploma for having finished jury service. But instead of feeling ecstatic, I felt like garbage. I had gamed a system I believed in my whole life.

Driving home, I saw four police cars surrounding three kids facing a wall, hands cuffed behind their backs. I'd be up for jury duty again in twelve months.

IT .
HAD TO HAPPEN
EVENTUALLY
MOVE ON
DOT .ORG

NOTES FROM THE SITCOM'S DEATHBED

■ ■

TUESDAY, AUGUST 19, 2003

Spent afternoon lolling around the DreamWorks animation campus in Glendale, California. The place is like Berkeley, warm and full-blooded with youth and grass and belief.

"Mehlman!"

Wheel around: It's Jonathan Berry, junior executive of DreamWorks Television.

"Peter, I was going to call you. It's almost pilot season."

Ignore the rumors. L.A. does have four seasons: earthquake season, fire season, riot season, and the most ravaging—pilot season. Network TV keeps groping to win over an America it despises—a viewing public it sees as a blurry, fat, brainless blob of uninsured, Hemi-powered, God-fearing Wal-Mart clerks. I'm paid to entertain them.

"When should I come by your office?"

"Two-thirty."

Jonathan races off. I turn, walk and bump into Jonathan's bosses, Darryl Frank and Justin Falvey. Both are mid-thirties, slick and smart. Makes you wonder why they chose not to contribute to society. I wonder that about myself. But that's our America: Harvard grads once wrote speeches for Jack Kennedy. Now it's dialogue for Jim Belushi.

We chat about ratings, producers, agents and a guy who fell victim to identity theft. I say, "No one has to steal my identity.

They can have it." Darryl laughs: "You gotta put that in a script!"

Sure. A funny line that doesn't end up in a sitcom. What good does that do anyone?

Justin says it's time for me to think up a new sitcom idea. Because the sitcom is like a terminally ill patient hanging on for no apparent reason, I want to say I'd rather be a travel agent on the Gaza Strip, but Justin gets a cell call.

I get an idea for a sitcom: 77 Gaza Strip.

Two-thirty. Jonathan's office. "Oh, Mehlman, you didn't have to come over. Darryl and Justin told me they saw you. That's all I wanted to talk to you about."

"Okay."

"I'm sending you the Network Landscape."

"Landscape?"

"The listing of what kind of new shows the networks are looking for. I send it to you every year."

"Do I ever read it?"

"No."

WEDNESDAY, AUGUST 27

Today starts out as the kind of day I love. No plans. No meetings. Nothing. Still, I feel hemmed in, like the world will pop in at any moment. I have no wife, no kids, no responsibilities, and yet forty times a day I mutter to myself, "Christ, it never ends."

Outside a Starbucks in Santa Monica with my dog, Izzy, a mutt with so many warring instincts ping-ponging through her head she never knows whether to beg for treats or sniff suitcases for anthrax. At the next table are a man and four women.

Idea for sitcom: A woman gets divorced from a polygamist and collects alimony from one man and three women.

Turn the other way. A young girl is reading *The Autobiography of Malcolm X*.

Idea for sitcom: *The Autobiography of Malcolm in the Middle*.

God. Can't believe my mind works like this. Writing for *Seinfeld* turned my life into a research project, something to watch rather than live. After the Northridge earthquake extended the grueling 1993–94 *Seinfeld* season, I went to a spa in Tucson,

Arizona. It was Mother's Day weekend and the spa was overrun with mothers and daughters splurging on massages, wraps and all-over tans. Wound up hanging out with a daughter. On our last day, we started feverishly making out on a tiny bridge over a dry streambed. In the heat of the action, I thought to myself: *It's amazing how every girl has her own kissing system*. Right hand here, left hand there, top lip doing this, bottom lip that. No two the same.

How's that for spectating your own life?

Go home and shower. Wonder if you can learn French purely from shampoo bottles. The DreamWorks guys call to set a meeting at 6 p.m. tomorrow. Ten minutes later, my assistant, Chi, calls to tell me I have a meeting with "the boys" at 6 p.m. tomorrow. An hour later, the boys call to move the meeting up to 3. Chi calls: The meeting is moved to 3. The boys call to push the meeting back to 5:15. Chi calls: "5:15." Another call. "Make it 2:45." Chi: "2:45."

Finally, it's decided the meeting can be a conference call. Showing up is an idea whose day has come and gone.

Should have asked what they want to talk about during the conference call.

THURSDAY, AUGUST 28

Starbucks. At the next table, a father and daughter. "Daddy, you can lead an active life. Look at Dick Cheney. He's vice president, and he's had God knows how many 'heart episodes.'"

Good point. Cheney has had enough heart episodes to go into syndication.

Back home for the conference call. Justin says, "So, what's your idea for your next pilot?"

Oh. So that's what this call is about. My idea for a pilot. Already? Wow. I have nothing. This is bad. Really bad.

Stalling, I yell, "Izzy, stop it!" even though she's sleeping two feet away from me with her favorite toy, a purple rubber squeaky shoe.

Izzy. Shoe... reminds me of something that happened just before lunch today.

I start talking: "Okay, uh, I guess I should start by telling you the genesis of my idea for my next pilot. I was walking on

Montana Avenue after lunch a few, um, weeks ago—many weeks ago—when my dog poked her head in a women's shoe store. Inside, I saw this clearly gay man selling shoes to a woman who was listening intently to everything he said. So I thought to myself, 'Wouldn't it be funny if that guy weren't gay? That he was just putting on an act because women trust gay salesmen?'"

Justin: "That's hysterical!"

Darryl: "So funny!"

Huh.

Me: "So, um, what I was thinking was, well, doing a show about this character—a young kid, handsome, maybe twenty-two—who will do anything to make it. Anything. He'll scam, act, lie, wear disguises—nothing illegal, of course—but he will do anything just to, you know, get ahead. Just to make it. To make it in America."

Justin: "That's a great character."

Jonathan: "Yeah, totally different."

Darryl: "Is there a female character?"

Me: "Oh, of course there's, um, a female character. She's, uh—sorry, I can't read my own notes. Oh, right: She's the woman he was selling the shoes to! An older woman. Not old, but older. Like, oh... Heather Locklear! Well, anyway, she's also got this drive to 'make it,' only she's getting a late start because she was married for twelve years and just got divorced from her rich husband who had a low sperm count and wound up cheating with their female fertility doctor because, you know, how women will do anything not to have to use birth control? Anyway, Heather Locklear finds out the kid isn't gay and gets him fired. But then she feels guilty. Blah, blah, blah, they wind up going into business together. The scamming kid, the older—but really hot!—woman. And there's sexual tension there! Like that whole Ashton Kutcher-Demi Moore pandemic! But, but, but, but that's only a side aspect of the show. The main theme is making it in America. It's a classic American story, but we haven't seen anything like it on TV—not that there's anything on TV that resembles American life but—still, that's the show. The show is that. It's, it's, it's, it's... a modern-day version of The Great Gatsby!"

The DW boys flip out.

Darryl: "The kid is such a great character, any actor would kill for the part."

Justin: "Mehlman, I can't believe you already put so much thought into this!"

Jonathan: "We were betting that you wouldn't have anything."

Justin: "Take the rest of the week off."

End of conference call.

Okay. So I can make a sitcom out of thin air. Yippee. Actually, I've had other, richer sitcom-provoking moments lately. Just yesterday, I saw two black men talking in Century City. They both wore suits, so naturally I assumed they were from the Nation of Islam. I walked over to them and said, "Hi. Salaam alaikum. I was just wondering—I know as Muslims you don't eat pork, but, out of curiosity, does it anger you that pork is now referred to as 'the other white meat'?"

Okay, so I didn't say that. But I thought it. And that would make a funny sitcom: *The Accidental Racist*. No, too specific. How about *Faux Pas*? Better yet: *Gaffe*. The networks think one-word titles make for the best sitcoms. With all their research and focus groups, that's what they've concluded. One-word titles are good. Gives one the sense that network TV's main dilemma is "How can we get around this quality problem?"

I call my new pilot *Dash*.

MONDAY, SEPTEMBER 1

Walked Izzy late last night. This morning, on my kitchen counter, was a New York Times bag filled with dog shit. The point is, my mind wanders.

Drove a friend to LAX. Happy clots of postcollegiate radio/TV/film majors stream out of terminals, pumped and dreamy. The show-business in-box is always flooded.

At *Seinfeld*, we got crate loads of spec-script submissions. The show's situations were so real, people felt as if their lives could be episodes. So they wrote scripts, mailed them in, and waited for fat checks and thin Writer's Guild cards. After a few lawsuits charging we stole ideas we didn't steal, Castle Rock—the show's production company—made us return all specs unread. To acknowledge the work and hope invested in these scripts, I wrote a thoughtful, apologetic boilerplate rejection letter. One season, the only state that didn't have a resident submit a *Seinfeld* script was Idaho. Michigan alone was responsible for more than seventy. Eight from Oklahoma, two from North Dakota, and more than thirty Missourians sat in their homes writing about four New Yorkers who had no clue about what it was like to live in the rest of America.

Once, when people felt the urge to write, they wrote books or stories or plays. TV was a high-paying reward you fell into after years of high-quality, low-paying writing coupled with the backlogging of life experiences not substantial enough for a novel but fine for television—like beef going to the Alpo warehouse instead of The Palm. Now it's a beeline from college to laugh-sweetened dialogue. And not witty, 1590-on-my-SATs dialogue. See, networks aren't solely responsible for horrid sitcoms. Writers are the unindicted co-conspirators.

You'd think people who want to write would aspire to their own level of greatness. But sitcom writers don't want to write; they want to be in show business. Luckily, most never have to write. Life is spent in a room all night barking out jokes. If one of the jokes sticks to that day's draft of the script, you proudly get to call yourself a writer. You and Philip Roth and Joan Didion and Thomas Pynchon, writers. Your name gets on scripts that you were in the vicinity of, like Derek Jeter getting the call despite never touching the bag when turning the double play. Of course, Derek Jeter could touch the bag if he needed to. Most sitcom writers couldn't knock together a suicide note without help from a roomful of twenty-two-minute personalities.

"Guys, can you punch up my suicide note? It's just... lying there."

Before the '90s went out of business, being on a hit show was hitting the lottery. Pre-*Seinfeld*, I'd barely written any dialogue in my life. Just as I was clueing in to foreign concepts like "dramatic structure," production companies swarmed to sign me to multimillion-dollar contracts. A first-year MBA student would have vomited at the lack of research behind the offers. People threw money at me to create a hit show for them without ever asking, "Do you have any ideas?" It was lovely, but I vaguely wanted to justify it, to state my case, to say that *Seinfeld* was the only show in which you came up with your own story lines or you were gone. There was no "writers' room." You wrote and rewrote your own scripts before kissing them off to Larry David and Jerry so they could dose it with magic. I was ready to say I did bad work on "The Visa," better on "The Sponge," really good on "The Implant." I was ready to argue that my episodes showed signs of a sensibility: A bunch dealt with radically changing one's appearance; a clump with contraception; a batch had people trying to be someone else; almost all had friends drastically at cross-purposes. My story lines were truly "about nothing." (Except when they weren't: It took me weeks to realize that my friend's experience with a valet parker's BO would make a funny episode. Too broad of an idea for me to see.)

Only DreamWorks personnel did their homework. They knew the episodes I'd written. They quoted lines. Sometimes I'd say, "Oh, that was actually Larry David's line," and they'd laugh it off as adorable modesty. The first time I met Jeffrey Katzenberg, I sat on a patio chair when Jeffrey came rushing out. As we were about to shake hands, he bonked his forehead into a metal lamp and gushed blood. "This is not good," I thought, "not good at all." Jeffrey calmly excused himself, then returned holding a white towel to his head. As I watched the towel steadily redden, Jeffrey said, "That Chinese Woman episode you wrote was brilliant. Donna Changstein changing her name to Chang to pass herself off as Chinese? Unbelievable! I'm going to the hospital now." Jeffrey got double-digit stitches, my agents bought him a football helmet, and we met again. He urged me to sign with DreamWorks, adding "I bled for you." He didn't have to. He was so honest, so above the crap, I loved him.

After two more years at *Seinfeld*, I left and created *It's like, you know . . .* for ABC. Our first day of shooting the pilot was the morning after *Seinfeld* shot its finale in April 1998. I stayed on the *Seinfeld* set until 1:30 a.m. before telling Jerry and Larry I had my own show to do. Jerry said, "Here's the baton, run with it." Larry said, "God, I feel like I'm sending my kid off to college."

Clearly I was a freshman. When ABC execs gave me their first note on the script—a small plot change—I pondered it and said, "No, I think it's good the way it is. What else you got?" The ABC brass looked at me as if I'd announced I was pro-pedophilia. My first experience with network interference. *Seinfeld* had no network interference because it was a show that fell through the cracks. In television, a great show that's canceled hasn't fallen through the cracks. A great show that thrives has fallen through the cracks.

It's like, you know ... shot twenty-six episodes before ABC canceled it to clear more time slots for *Who Wants To Be a Millionaire*. I mentioned that I wouldn't do another show for ABC if the future of Israel depended on it, and things got a little messy for me for a while, but everyone cooled down, and I realized I should've been shocked the show lasted as long as it did. It got great reviews—a bad thing. One network head stated on the record that well-reviewed shows are ratings losers and vice versa. The press bought into that. Twice a year, TV critics from all over the country come to L.A. to meet with TV producers—a chance for the lowest form of journalism to hobnob with the lowest form of art. During *ILYK*, critics kept asking if I worried about the show being "too smart." When the show was canceled, *TV Guide* asked me the same question in the past tense. I felt such rage ...

Until I felt such relief. A dirty secret: When a show is canceled, the show runner is always partly relieved. The work is brutal and gets more brutal as the season wears on. You're on the set so much, you have no life to write about. And if an idea does pop into your leaden head, there's hardly time to execute it. Once, needing to write an entire *ILYK ...* episode in a few hours ... I heard a deejay say that Paul McCartney took sixty-seven takes to record the song "I Will." A beautiful ditty barely two minutes long, sixty-seven takes. I got a few hours to muscle out twenty-two minutes of comedy.

* * *

After *ILYK ...* I was hot to do another show, so I wrote a pilot without telling anyone about it: *The White Album*, a dark, comic, serialized murder mystery. When people read it, they kept saying "It's sitcom *noir*—a whole new genre!" I saw it as *Airplane!* meets David Lynch. I'm proud to live in a country that allows David Lynch to make his movies.

The script went to networks. They loved it. They all rejected it. The reason, according to inside sources, was that the networks didn't have "creative ownership" over it. In less breathtakingly incoherent terms: Writing the show before telling them about it made them feel jilted. They weren't part of the creative process. You might wonder why someone who wants to be part of the creative process would become an executive as opposed to say, a writer. Pondering that kind of question is a giant waste of a sitcom writer's time. They want to be part of the creative process without being creative, and if they're not, they lose interest. It's been said that in the history of the world, no one ever washed a rented car. In TV, rented cars are totaled.

So next time, I played ball. I pitched a show about a gorgeous fifteen-year-old girl in Middle America who knows for a fact that, in a previous life, she was Sigmund Freud. She just wants to be a happy kid but can't fight her destiny. She constantly analyzes and helps people. She finally shares her secret with the only adolescent psychologist in town. He realizes she really was Freud, and they have this father-daughter-mentor-student-idol-fan relationship. Then I packaged the show in terms a network could understand: "It's like *My Favorite Martian* with a sexy girl instead of Ray Walston and a legendary genius instead of a Martian."

The networks loved it. Then rejected it.

Why?

Because they did not feel their audience would know who Freud was.

Yes, I'm serious.

Maybe I should have reincarnated Kurt Cobain. A *Seinfeld* episode dealt with John Cheever and people didn't tune out!

Then again, if your ratings are high enough, you can do a whole season about Noam Chomsky.

Odd thing . . . When I started pitching shows after *Seinfeld*, a stunning fact emerged: The networks hated *Seinfeld*. They liked it as fans, but professionally, they resented it. It broke all their rules about likable characters, setup/punch line dialogue, everything. It didn't fall into one of their comfort zones, like "a classic fish-out-of-water story!" And the fact that *Seinfeld* never had touching moments made the networks apoplectic.

Hey, you know when *Friends* finally won an Emmy for best comedy? When NBC promoted each episode with emotional moments drenched in mournful music by Enya. "Who can say where the road goes... ?" That is when *Friends* won an Emmy for best comedy. Really, *Friends* was more deserving of an Emmy for the achievement of being a monstrously popular show that, aside from Jennifer Aniston's hair, managed to avoid occupying one inch of America's cultural landscape.

Whatever. *Dash* won't have heartwarming moments.

Possibly because I won't allow it.

Probably because no network will ever air it.

EPILOGUE

On a Thursday, I verbally pitched *Dash* to NBC executives.

The following Tuesday, I called Justin to ask if he'd heard NBC's verdict. There was silence over the phone, and then he yelled: "Mehlman! What world are you in? NBC bought the show in the room—right in front of you!"

Oh. Guess I missed that part. I remember, during the meeting, I drifted off a while thinking that if I were president, I'd insist that all cars have the gas tank on the same side. That was probably the moment when NBC said they'd buy the show.

I really enjoyed writing the pilot. It's important to enjoy the writing because once you hand in your script, your linkage to joy loosens in the way a car devalues when you drive it off the lot.

E-mailed the script to DreamWorks. Bye.

Justin called from Glendale. Loved the script. Darryl called from Utah. Loved the script. Katzenberg called from his car. Loved the script.

NBC called from Ratingsville and rejected the script. With that call *Dash* died, and my DreamWorks deal ran out the following June.

Why did NBC reject *Dash*? This time, I didn't investigate why. A theory: When you pitch a show as "a modern-day version of *The Great Gatsby*," network people are embarrassed to reject both you *and* F. Scott Fitzgerald outright. So they buy it, you write it, then they can reject it, secure in the (false) impression they truly considered a high-minded situation comedy.

There: a theory, a postmortem, a rationalization—all mine— for why *Dash* died. A good assessment of why? A bad assessment of why? Not important. When you write sitcoms for a living, you treat yourself to whys you can live with.

L.A. — The Hedge-a-Dream Factory

■ ■

AT THE PLACE I LUNCH every day in an effort to cut down on life choices, I've been reading a Tolstoy-sized article in the *New Yorker* about Scientology. Nearly every day, some patron raids my airspace, saying something like, "I read that article." Eye roll, then, "What whack jobs."

L.A. finds Scientology so endlessly fascinating that weeks after publication, people are still talking about the article all over town. Why? Here's a theory: There is no city on Earth that makes rationalization more difficult than Los Angeles.

OK, here's an example.

Fifty or so lunches earlier, a man at the next table was fiercely editing a screenplay with three Sharpies: red, blue and black. When he paroled himself to the restroom, I peeked at the title page: UNTITLED. AN ORIGINAL SCREENPLAY BY [unfamiliar name]. A furtive IMDB search revealed a one-credit, straight-to-video film career.

Upon returning, Sharpie leaned toward another patron and said: "I love your work. But the last film... not so much."

As someone who looks away from train wrecks, I dove into an egg white and turkey bacon quesadilla and hatched the seed of my rationalization theory: People come to L.A. with big dreams, but every time we hedge a dream, there's someone or something in our sightline reminding us of that hedge. Our lost dream is someone else's reality, and that someone is everywhere—on billboards, in rearview mirrors, at the next table over a coffee so much more full-bodied than our own. Then, when we get skilled at deluding ourselves into thinking our pruned dreams are pretty fine, we sit in a dental office, open *In Style* and see all the parties to which we weren't invited.

Even if we can sidestep L.A.'s name-brand gods, there are total no-names pinpricking the bargains we've made with ourselves: Baristas, trainers and receptionists steal glances at their scripts or practice their monologues aloud in public. Yes, odds are they're blind to the oncoming reality that may soon tie the lap band around their future. But unlike us, they have the arrogance of people whose dreams are still intact.

It's very annoying. How do you cope when your city's soft underbelly has washboard abs?

The answer is, not well. We gossip, spread rumors and take passive-aggressive potshots at people eating lunch.

In no other city do citizens have such constant exposure to people living the lives we want. In this nation, there are dreamers and dreamees, but the dreamees in other cities are pretty much anonymous. In L.A., we know so much about the people living the lives we want, it's almost impossible to effectively rationalize our own failure: No, he's actually allergic to all women except his wife. No, she actually has a 179 IQ. No, he actually put forty-four million underprivileged children through college. No, without makeup, she actually has pores that can only be seen with an electron microscope. No, actually, he doesn't put his pants on one leg at a time. According to *Us Weekly*, he pulled on both pant legs simultaneously.

And yet, most adults live in L.A. by choice. In fact, it's the first of many, many choices we made in a city offering way too many choices. To maintain self-esteem and sanity, we desperately grope for something that makes us feel good about our choices. Rationalization is all we have, and this all adds up to a real civic problem.

* * *

Okay, you're thinking, how does the Scientology obsession connect to all this?

Well, let's face it: Scientology discovered celebrity marketing way before Nike. Some of our biggest megastars are members. However, one unintended backwash is that Scientology provides a great service to L.A.'s Judeo-Christian, rationalization-starved citizenry. We can consider (oh, let's say) Tom Cruise with his epic career, then remind ourselves that despite having a beautiful planet in the palm of his hand, he belongs to a religion that is, according to any reading of the *New Yorker* article, berserk.

Ah, now we feel better. Our aspirations may be sold and resold, but at least we don't belong to a religion that asks some of its members to sign contracts lasting a billion years.

We will stop short of pondering the sanity of burning bushes, parted seas and forty-year walks through the desert well before the advent of bottled water.

In L.A., the whiff of one workable rationalization, no matter how flimsy, is a sweet anesthetic.

RAISING MODERATELY HEALTHY JERKS

■ ■

ONE FOGGY NIGHT IN LOS Angeles I attended a party for a big birthday, one of the years when the very industry employing most of the guests sweeps you out of all demographic relevance. One clot of five or so guests stood around discussing a great man and eating one of eighty dishes featuring truffle oil. There was a general consensus that this was a great man. Not Mandela great, but run-of-the-mill great. You know, friendly, charitable, good-hearted, socially conscious... show-biz greatness.

Someone like, say, Martin Sheen.

However, at a certain point, a dreary *Oh, wait a sec...* fell over the discussion because this great man does have a (talented, successful) kid who's led a spectacularly tawdry life, even by Hollywood standards.

One attendee, in the voice of someone making a ransom demand: "Sure, he's great—but he couldn't have been a very great father."

A hush. The attendee put his arm around his famine-chic wife, who nodded and confirmed, "Had to be a really bad father."

The idiocy here doesn't live only in the media-fueled presumption of the great man's poor parenting skills. It also lives in the apparent fact that a person's life—no matter how accomplished, influential, or generous he is; no matter how much joy his life has provided the world—is dashed by the judgment of parenthood. Does being a bad parent trump all?

At this very moment (and now this moment, and this moment), there are, let's say, five million people in America who are saying the following words: "Being a parent is the hardest job in the world."

They may be right. But if it's so difficult, why is a person's entire being automatically and permanently blackened and voided for being a *bad* parent?

Neurosurgery. That's a hard job, too. There are probably medical school kids who tried but couldn't adequately reconnect a severed wrist. Those kids are advised—encouraged!—to try a different specialty. When they take up endocrinology or epidemiology, their ineptitude with the central nervous system will be forgiven. They'll lead lives of great esteem.

(Unless they're also bad parents.)

Coal mining. Another tough job. Oh, skip that for now.

This Bad Parent Syndrome casts a gargantuan shadow. A walk on any street or scan of any newspaper reveals endless amounts of overtly objectionable people. Some of their deficiencies undoubtedly sprung from dismal childhoods at the hands of one or two (or three or four) inept/neglectful/fill-in-the-blank parents. Summarily dumping all of those parents from the ranks of decent human beings and ignoring the rest of their existence not only is harsh but vaguely smacks of the same traits that made these people bad parents to begin with.

The inverse of Bad Parent Syndrome is equally whacked. The day before Bernie Madoff's son committed suicide, rest assured, someone on the Upper East Side of New York said, "You know, despite it all, Bernie Madoff was a really good father."

If you're a good parent, you cannot be all bad. On the other hand, if you're Paul Newman and you entertain billions of people, establish a mega-successful company in which all profits go to charity, but have a son who over-dosed—sorry, Paul, only the puniest of mitigating graces for you.

This annihilating attitude has been quadrupled as the Baby Boomers and gen X-ers come of age. The population bulge that invented the concept of blaming their foibles on their parents, and the ensuing psycho-boomlet that perfected it. Good God, what's more grinding than hearing siblings repeatedly run down the blow-by-blow evolution of their parentally inflicted damage? (Uh, where was I at the dinner table when all this incessant abuse was taking place?) Somehow, the same generations—the self-satisfied parents who announce that raising kids is the hardest thing they've ever done—can't look at their own parents and say, "Hey, it's a hard job. They tried the best they could." Then again, the life-long vilification of their own parents is undoubtedly the seed of the venom they direct toward their imperfect peers.

The fascinating outgrowth of all this is that there is now an ever-widening, bazillion-dollar growth industry devoted to trying to make bad parenting almost impossible. No matter what symptom or aberrant behavior your kid exhibits, there is a diagnosis to tell you, "It's not your fault." Biting, punching, bullying, cutting, bulimia, anorexia, obesity, illiteracy... you name it, there is an FDA-approved, NIH-researched acronym to explain it and get you off the hook because, in the final analysis, you really are good at the hardest job in the world and don't let anyone tell you different.

And maybe you shouldn't let anyone tell you any different. The greatest parenting in the history of the world guarantees very little. Good at the job, bad at the job, indifferent at the job, we all know luck plays a gigantic role in how a child turns out. There are so many unnoticed moments that can tip the seesaw the other way that it's impossible to rate one's job performance. There are so many influences raining down from all angles that, the job defies qualification. There are so many chemicals and enzymes and radioactive waves that you don't even know about when you're on the job.

There are some horrendously bad parents out there. Some are so bad they deserve condemnation. But there are also some bad parents who try their best and are just naturally unsuited for the job. They may know it or they may not. But no matter how undeniably good at the job someone is, deep down, every parent knows it takes a lot of good fortune to raise even a moderately healthy jerk, no less a well-adjusted pillar of the community with exceptional parenting skills.

SIX HUNDRED CHOICE WORDS FOR THE CHATTERERS

■ ■

TO THE COUPLE WHO TALKED throughout the entire 7:30 show-ing of *Crash* in Westwood: I thought e-mail could be a refreshing-ly civil tack in dealing with such moths in the fabric of society as yourselves. After all, the only cliché worse than talking during a movie is yelling at the people doing the talking.

So, in lieu of invoicing you for 113 minutes of my life, I'm letting you know—sweetly—that during the movie, you TALKED EVERY #%&*@ SECOND. (Sorry, my caps stick sometimes.)

Judging from the flakes of Dolby Digital sound that sneaked past your conversation, *Crash* seemed to be about cop-ing with deeply flawed individuals in Los Angeles. How's that for coincidence?

Here's a bigger coincidence: Profiling seemed to be anoth-er theme of *Crash*, and you neatly fit that of a movie-talker: Long-married couple who check Blackberries during the movie but don't share popcorn, arm rests or enough common interests any-more to carry on a conversation in your empty nest, which one of you wants to sell now before real estate prices tank because you're worried about how you'll continue putting brioche on the table during the agonizing slow slog of your golden years.

So you go to the movies. To talk. It's easier there. It's dark.

This kind of talking prevents other viewers from being en-grossed in a film—especially a film often described as "engross-ing." Also, many people, when attending a film, like to hear the dialogue. It helps in the matter of grasping the plot. The characters' lips moved, so why not, these people feel, have the whole movie-going experience?

Not that your dialogue wasn't engrossing. Truly, there was a moment late in the film's first act—let's say page 25 of the script—when it was tempting to ask if you could speak up so you could be heard over the movie. In addition, twice during the showing, the man in your relationship could be heard using the word "verisimilitude." Both times he said this word, his bald, (Mr. Potato) head tilted to the left in, one can only guess, an effort at emphasis. But the real intrigue lies in why he threw around a word that survives only on the pages of writers who try too hard. He wasn't trying to impress you, the woman in the relationship. Presumably, you've heard him go mega-syllabic a million times. So, he must have said "verisimilitude" for the benefit of those sitting around him.

Odd thing... In L.A., we have freeway shootings but no movie-audience shootings. Cars and movies are our biggest loves. It stands to reason. . . . Wait. Sorry. Forget that. I lost track of my civility for a second.

Funny how that happens, losing one's civility, despite being constantly reminded how to act around others. Take, for example... in movie theaters. After the trailers, theater owners give us detailed instructions on how to watch a movie. "Silence is golden," they say. What do they take us for? Idiots?

Then again, maybe they just take us for good God-fearing Americans who want to enjoy our two-hour break from making America great. That would explain a lot. Here in left-wing L.A., we allegedly don't fear God. At most, God makes us edgy. Hence: We can talk during movies. Who is He—or Loews Cineplex—to stop us?

Odd thing... My dad was in the hospital recently. The man in the next bed (we referred to him as my dad's "rheummate") asked whether his heart monitor was too loud for my dad to hear the TV. Can you be too considerate? No, you cannot.

Not to say that you two could take a lesson from the rheummate. But you two could take a lesson.

Anyway, I just read a review of Crash and I guessed right: It did deal with L.A. situations such as the one we are dealing with now.

You're thinking: How's that for verisimilitude?

I'm thinking: Take an ad out in this newspaper whenever you go to a movie so the rest of the world can plan accordingly.

THE MIDDLE OF SOMEWHERE—
WHY I HATE TO TRAVEL

■ ■

IT'S A LITTLE EARLY TO call it a phenomenon or a syndrome or even a drift, but when admitting that I hate travel, people seem slower to write me off as a listless, incurious slug. With more conversation, I can usually bring them around to that conclusion, but travel aversion alone doesn't smirch like it used to.

Ten years ago, disliking travel branded you under some dullard's version of Megan's Law. The admission hot-wired people's nervous systems: eyes zoomed in and dollied out on you; delete buttons fired in whatever part of the brain controls dinner-party invitations; body language suddenly spoke fluent English: You hate travel? You *hate* travel? You hate *travel*?

Yes and yes and yes but . . . times are changing. People seem more tolerant of the hunkered down. They've gained empathy for inertia freaks. Some have even slouched toward the "stay-cation," a handy detour around the shame of parochialism. Not long ago at a super high-thread-count dinner party in Martha's Vineyard (Okay, I went to Martha's Vineyard—I'll explain later), a woman said to me, "I still like traveling, but sometimes it's like marriage . . . not all it's cracked up to be." Half jokingly, or three-eighths jokingly, I replied that I didn't know *either* were cracked up to be much and . . . she smiled. No really, I'm pretty sure she smiled.

At first knee jerk, reasons for a travel backlash are splashing everywhere: recession, 9/11, gas, brawny Euros, scrawny dollars, malaria, aisle seat fees, security gate shoe-removal. "One whacko booby-traps his Nikes, and we have to remove our shoes for eternity? It's sick." Yes, getting there is half the agony.

Popular bothers aside, my travel problem is more internal: I just don't like going anywhere. As an aspiring agoraphobic, I like being home. The sweet habit of home holds life's potential. Preferring to be available to my own life, I'm pretty sure news about an optioned screenplay won't reach me in Tuscany. It doesn't reach me in Santa Monica either, but at least here, self-delusion makes some sense. Other people may like being in the middle of nowhere. Not me. And my atlas shows maybe four places in the world that aren't in the middle of nowhere.

And yet, people continue to ask, what about daring adventure? Well, when wars break out, I do envy those action-junkie photojournalists snapping away through sniper fire then hurdling headlong into desperate combat romances, but those aren't the adventures we're discussing here. We're on the level of an Antarctic eco-tour, which is just running away from oneself for two weeks of life on gelid hold. And anyway, as Eudora Welty said, "all serious daring starts from within." Granted, just because Eudora Welty said it doesn't mean it's true, but in this case, I really think she was on to something.

People also ask about the oxymoronic concept of a pleasure trip (and I'm not so sure of the oxy part). Here, the implications are twofold: Home lacks pleasure, a dreary scenario only exacerbated by resorts with better amenities than your own home, and a change of scenery does a person good. In Normandy (okay, I went to Normandy), I learned that the French refer to such travel as a way to *change les idees*—change your ideas. Granted, just because the French say it doesn't mean it's wrong, but in this case, I really think they're wrong.

Case in point, a few years ago, fleets of L.A.'s yoga demons lugged their purple mats to India precisely to *change les idees*. I was asked along on several such trips but declined. India is no doubt fascinating, and the people sound very nice over the phone but... thanks for asking and Godspeed. As it turned out, the only changes in ideas I heard from returning travelers dealt with multiplying the recommended dosage of Imodium. The best idea was an advanced formula called Explodium.

On the upside, I learned enough about about India to close my eyes and convince myself I'd gone there and never needed to go back. One imagined trip was enough. Really, it's staggering how much you can learn about the world by avoiding it. Without moving a muscle, I know St. Bart's is "so restful," Machu Pinchu "so transcendant" and the Masai "so cheerful." I don't see why I have to confirm it all first hand. You've rated the hotels, reviewed the meals, described the felonious cab drivers . . . why see the movie?

Which exposes another dimly lit truth: the high point of any trip is when it's over. People like travel but they love saying, "I just got back from Uruguay." With open access to exotic locales, travel has become a seedy form of exhibitionism, more something to recount than experience. I know this because I'm as guilty as anyone.

A few years ago I went on what others referred to as "a vacation" to Vietnam. (Okay, I also went to Vietnam) Back in L.A., everyone got a dose of "I just got back from Vietnam." They'd ask how I enjoyed the trip and I'd say, "Actually, I don't know what all those Vietnam veterans were whining about. . . . I had a great time."

I suddenly felt like an intriguing person. Really, if I could just say stuff like that without bothering to go anywhere, travel could become a real passion for me.

* * *

As evidenced from the mentions of Martha's Vineyard, Normandy and Vietnam, I do travel some. In recent years, I've also been to Norway, Denmark, Israel, a slew of ski resorts and Syracuse in February. And just before it became a museum piece, I took the Concorde to Paris.

I think that's pretty much—no, wait, I've also taken a few trips to Mexico. (Idea for resort in Afghanistan: Kabul San Lucas.) So yes, hating travel doesn't necessarily preclude it.

In fact, Martha's Vineyard was part of an effort to hate travel less: A year or so ago, I bought a little home there. Without getting too deeply into it, at the point of purchase, I hadn't seen the house. Nor had I ever been to Martha's Vineyard, a place that seemed a long way to go to see the same people I can see dining at Giorgio's in Santa Monica every night. Yet, the idea of a vacation home sounded like a way to be away and home at the same time. On my first visit, it was almost exactly like being home: meandering days, dinner with friends at night. By the fifth dinner party, I was starting to run a little low on personality but overall, the whole trip wasn't at all overtly horrific. And I got to tell people, "I just got back from Martha's Vineyard."

As for the other trips, honestly, I'm not totally sure how they happened. If I had to pinpoint something, I'd say the thing that gets me on a plane, more often than not, is sheer stupidity. Stupidity and inexplicable lapses in self-awareness. I commit to trips far in advance when they're not quite real, when it's not me going so much as some future me. Let him worry about Oslo. Most places have appeal from a distance of six months, and until the flights are booked, it's all just theory anyhow. Of course, in about thirty seconds, the trip is a week away and reality crashes in.

The week before a trip is like imminent death: Home will still be here, I'll be gone. My last trip to Starbuck's before a trip feels like my last trip to Starbuck's. It's not fear of flying or dying; the annihilating dread is nonspecific. Somehow, a return to my blessed day-to-day-iety seems out of reach. Those eight days, seven nights become a wall blocking out life in the way final exams used to block out summer, only less dopey.

But a commitment's a commitment, so after waiting until the last second to book the trip in the hope that the State Department will suddenly declare Paris unsafe for Americans, I pay the maximum possible airfare, assuming that survival is included in the price.

Once at the destination, I often experience a dram of dissociative pleasure. Wow, you're actually in Saigon. This kind of wonder is a gateway drug leading to a breakfast of quail eggs and some day-trip on a hydrofoil or a six-seat crop duster. That's when I snap back to me, silently chanting, I'd rather be anywhere else in the world right now. Anywhere. Atlantic City. Houston. A Knicks game. Walking through Baghdad wearing a yarmulke.

Chastened, the rest of the trip is devoted to running out the clock, a cautiously optimistic, passport-hugging vigil of bland meals, prepaid taxis and yearning phone calls to my home planet.

On return to LAX, I'm an improbably freed hostage walking off the plane on boneless legs, primed to kiss American soil. Luckily, we land on tarmac so I don't have to. Instead, I swear to never go anywhere again, to be nostalgic for home life as I live it.

In the cab ride home, the question, "Why travel?" rivals the question "Is there a God?" Such a mystery, this desire to budge.

Back home, a brochure from The World Wildlife Fund touts a two-week voyage of discovery to the Galapagos Islands. I toss it in the recycle bin, thinking, *maybe if they run an eco-tour of Westwood...*

COLD CASE FILES—O.J. SIMPSON

■ ■

NOVEMBER COMES TOWARD THE END of the year in Brentwood and yet another fog of the O.J. Simpson case loomed over the affluent town like a portobello mushroom cloud.

Trying to keep focused, Litton Wynn, Jr., L.A.P.D. cold case detective/music consultant, puzzled over a six-year-old littering case. His only physical evidence was a crumpled paper, which, on a hunch, he uncrumpled. With the aid of a forensic stationer, he IDed the item as a self-addressed envelope. Then he glanced at the return address: 771 Bundy.

Wynn's blood ran cold. He put on earmuffs and let his memory drift back . . . first to the summer of '94 when the Simpson case broke, and then to the autumn of '88 when nothing much really happened.

Wynn had wanted to reopen the Simpson investigation in '97 but sensed some resistance when his commanding officer suspended him for half an hour without pay. The boss was playing hardball, but it didn't scare Wynn. He'd once been a catcher in the White Sox organization. He considered reopening the case again in '04 but took a bike ride instead.

Now Simpson was opening his mouth again, and, along with the envelope from Bundy, Wynn took it as a sign. Needing a stiff one, he got a baguette at the Bellwood Bakery, then rapped on his CO's door. The boss was all smiles as Brentwood had been named "Best American Town to Kill Someone" by Ladies' Home Journal.

Wynn said he wanted to reopen the Simpson investigation. This time, he got the answer he wanted: "Go ahead. Who gives a crap?"

Wynn was pumped. At the time of the murders, June 12, 1994, he'd been working an unsolved murder/jaywalking case. He was finally moved to the Simpson investigation on July 4 but had to attend a cookout and couldn't start until the ninth. By then, all the good clues were taken.

Now he got right to work, paying a visit to the home of former District Attorney Gil Garcetti. But Garcetti shook his head and said it was no use: he'd gone over the Simpson case in his mind a million times, then lent it to his niece who misplaced it.

Luckily, as Wynn walked out, Garcetti's family geologist stopped him: "I hear there's evidence at Toscana."

Toscana is a restaurant, an industry haunt on San Vicente. Wynn drove over and strong-armed the chef who nervously spilled some Chianti, then his guts. Turns out, a day after the murders, the chef tipped off Mark Fuhrman about a blood-stained knife he'd found in his oven mitt, but the detective couldn't get a reservation and never followed up.

The chef handed Wynn the knife. He asked C.S.I. to run tests on it, but the show was on hiatus. Ultimately, the knife was filched from the evidence room and returned to Toscana where it's still used to mince salmon.

But Wynn noticed something odd on Toscana's menu: "Ahi salad with Bibb lettuce and a woman at 362 Rockingham who can blow the Simpson case wide open; served as appetizer or entrée."

Next door to Simpson's former home, Wynn found Alma Larch, an eighty-two-year-old actress who starred in both A and B movies, compiling an overall GPA of 3.2. She told him a story.

"Two days after the murders, I found a bloody glove under my mentholyptus tree. I assumed it was O.J.'s because he was a Negro. I called the police but they said, 'Who cares about one glove? If you don't have a matching set, it's just stupid.'"

Alma removed the blood-caked glove from its Lucite display case. Wynn sent it to the crime lab, which found blood traces matching the DNA of Simpson, his murdered wife Nicole Brown Simpson, and also that of former president Harry Truman. But when Wynn asked for the glove back, the lab tech said he'd given it to former prosecutor Chris Darden. "He already had the other glove so I figured..."

Wynn traced Darden to the Coffee Bean on Barrington, where he was preparing for a guest shot on the sitcom Two and a Half Men. Wynn grabbed Darden, roughed him up, ran some lines with him, then asked for the glove.

"Okay, I'll level with you," Darden said. "The night before I introduced the glove in court, I wanted to make a good impression so I washed it. Later, I remember thinking, *since when does leather shrink?*"

Wynn asked for both gloves but Darden said he'd returned them to Fred Segal's for a store credit. Wynn sped over but the checkout girl had just sold the gloves to a lapsed vegan.

Wynn groaned, but the checkout girl smiled and said, "My friend Betsy saw O.J. driving like a maniac on Bundy the night of the murders."

Wynn found Betsy Lee at Maha Yoga on 26th. She was the all-American girl: Asian, with a body that didn't take coffee breaks. She said while driving on Bundy on the night of the murders, a white Bronco sped away from the curb in front of her. Betsy was sure it was O.J. and wrote down his license number because there was blood all over him and he didn't use his turn signal. The next day, she told her story to a detective. But when she mentioned she had a boyfriend, the detective threatened to report her to the INS. Betsy told him she was born in Westwood, but the detective didn't care and had her deported to San Diego. It took six years for her to get back to L.A. and another three hours to get her life back together.

Betsy shrugged: "Hey, my story's nothing next to that Millstone guy who videotaped the whole murder."

For a Baptist minister, Hugh Millstone was a decent amateur cinematographer. His shots of O.J. stabbing his victims won't threaten Hitchcock's status, but then, Hitch was a genius. Screening the murders on a fifty-six-inch plasma, Millstone recounted how he'd brought the tape to the police but they wouldn't accept it because it wasn't rewound to the beginning.

Wynn snapped, then booked a flight to Miami.

He found O.J. Simpson on the fifteenth hole at Doral. Wynn had attended some of the Simpson trial, once getting close enough to tell him his shirt was inside out, so now Simpson recognized him. "Detective," Simpson said, "you look *kinohoura* good." Wynn blushed then told Simpson about the knife, the glove, the tape, everything. Simpson took a gimme from the green side of the bunker and said his research for his book had turned up the same clues. "As far I can tell," Simpson said, "all the evidence points to me."

Flying back to L.A., Wynn had time to reflect. He was born to do cold case work—he'd spent his youth investigating the reasons why his parents had affixed "Jr." to his name even though his father's name was Ricky. At fourteen, when he confronted his father with a latex fiber from a Persian rug, his old man quickly confessed to being an asshole. Even then, Wynn had instincts that couldn't be learned. That's why he called them "instincts." But now, the Simpson case made Wynn question the meaning of his life.

(Not his whole life, just his work.)

(Not that his home life was so hot either.)

Back in L.A., Wynn drove to Bundy and gazed at the crime scene for what seemed like forty-five minutes but was actually forty-five minutes on the button. He decided to drop the Simpson case because he was double-parked. Besides, there another case was eating at him.

He went to his CO to reopen the Yasser Arafat case. His CO said, "Could you be any more predictable?"

Wynn said "thanks" and went home. He drew a bath, which came out looking more like a sketch, but no matter. There was work to do: Arafat lives in a bombed-out office in the occupied territories for years, then finally takes a vacation in Paris and turns up dead within a week?

No way, thought Wynn. No way.

Zuckerman Juiced

■ ■

Santa Monica, Calif. — Not to cast aspersions but, with all of the furor over performance-enhancing drugs, it's remarkable that Philip Roth's name hasn't surfaced. Just last week Rafael Palmeiro avoided perjury charges, but his career achievements have been irreparably tarnished. Not so Roth. In fact, since turning sixty, an age when most renowned writers start having trouble making stuff up, Roth has written, arguably, four of his finest novels. Is he juiced or merely the beneficiary of superior genes? No one can— or will—say for sure.

However, as Roth closes in on several of Dostoevsky's records, whispers are circulating through the literary community. One writer, who requested anonymity to avoid seeming cranky, whispered, "Since I came out with *The Bonfire of the Vanities*, I've written two novels. Roth has churned out, what, twelve? Do the math."

Roth's bulked-up output is not the only factor raising eyebrows. Most notably, his sentence structure has shown no signs of the usual age-related deterioration cited in medical literature. At sixty-four, some eight to ten years after most writers betray noticeable passive voice, Roth completed his Pulitzer Prize–winning novel *American Pastoral* (1997). One of the book's astonishing sentences began with the words, "Only after strudel and coffee," and ended nearly a full page later without even one dangling modifier. No less a talent than James Joyce (in one of his more piquant observations) said: "By the age of forty-five, I knew I could no longer start a sentence with a mention of strudel. My fingers would want to do it, but my mind just wouldn't react."

In addition, Roth's continued graphic depiction of, and obsession with, sexuality is seen by some as another indicator that he may be doping. Even D. H. Lawrence, by the age of forty-two, tended to write less about sex and more about supper. Yet, Roth's *Sabbath's Theater* (1995) and *The Dying Animal* (2001) were rife with carnal observations usually associated with novelists freshly called up from the Iowa Writers' Workshop.

Roth's defenders point out that he lives in an age of superior mental conditioning, allowing him to extend his productive years well beyond that of Cervantes or the Grimm Brothers. (Cervantes was quick to admit he was no Cal Ripken, but he did stay in decent shape.) In addition, Roth has never fallen into the kinds of traps that have cut short the careers of others. He has displayed none of the draining machismo of Norman Mailer. He is never haunted by his childhood like Eugene (the Real Deal) O'Neill. He has no reputation for the late-night carousing favored by the likes of F. Scott Fitzgerald, Truman Capote and Bo Belinsky.

Finally, technology in the form of "spell-checker" and the "light bulb" have given Roth an advantage over, say, Rousseau. Some feel it would be foolish of him to forgo such labor-saving devices simply to maintain fair comparisons to the early Romantics. "Writing is hard," said one famously blocked author, who requested anonymity in order to keep her publisher believing she died twelve years ago. "You look for any edge you can get."

And yet, the dull hum of innuendo may become an annoying hum as volumes of Roth's work are reprinted by the prestigious Library of America. In an irony befitting the writings of O. Henry and Jose Canseco, much of the criticism for this controversy could ultimately land at the feet of that august imprint, whose testing has been so notably lax that Hunter S. Thompson repeatedly came up clean.

Thus far, Roth has been spared the kind of public denials to which we've grown accustomed. When a bottle of Allegorical Growth Hormone turned up in a Nebraska junior high school creative writing class, Roth was almost conspicuously not asked to comment on his status as a role model.

In short, Philip Roth simply lets his writing speak for itself. As one literary agent said: "You can dope me up all day, and I ain't going to write *Goodbye Columbus*. So when the time comes, I, for one, will write in Philip Roth for the *Time* magazine 100 Best Authors issue."

DeBakey's Heart

■ ■

IN THIRD GRADE, I WROTE a fan letter to Dr. Michael E. DeBakey. That sentence alone is baggy with implications: In 1964, there were actually doctors famous for being wonderful, as opposed to later, when our best known doctors would be named Kevorkian and Phil. In 1964, medicine was still magical, not just another corporate field best avoided. And in 1964, my mother was doing a bang-up job pushing me toward a career in medicine.

Dozens of factors contributed to my becoming the esteemed cardiologist I am not today. DeBakey, who died Friday at age ninety-nine, wasn't one of them.

According to family lore, my letter was oppressively cute in all its barely legible, science-y curiosity about the artificial heart DeBakey had famously pioneered. The prospect of their son dedicating his life to sloshing around chest cavities impelled my parents to spring for an airmail stamp, and off to Houston the letter flew. The response flew back to Queens just as fast. Yes, that's right. DeBakey, the superstar heart surgeon who was doing stuff like boosting an artery from a patient's leg and reassigning it to the same patient's thorax, took the time to write back.

DeBakey thanked me for my interest in his work and included literature featuring unbelievably cool photos of the surgically repaired gizzards deep inside some kind of cattle. I read the stuff like it was a collection of "Archie" comics.

The sixties media covered all of DeBakey's exploits. His heart procedures ran neck and neck with the space race for national fascination. Somewhere above my head, there seemed to be some feud going on between him and another superstar surgeon named Denton Cooley. I took sides like it was Mets versus Yankees. Then a South African surgeon named Christiaan Barnard did a heart transplant on a man named Louis Washkansky. Yes, healthcare was such a turn-on then that I still remember the name of the first transplant patient. I was disappointed that this foreign doctor nudged DeBakey out of the scrubs limelight, but DeBakey was lavish in his praise of Barnard, so I went along.

After some dizzyingly hopeful post-op reports of his sitting up and talking, Washkansky died eighteen days after his transplant. It felt like losing the World Series.

One day in 1969, my mother unexpectedly picked me up from junior high. "What are you doing here?" I asked. She said she was taking me to St. John's University to see a speech delivered by DeBakey. In a weird bit of reverse snobbery, I couldn't believe that DeBakey would come to New York.

After his speech, my mom pushed me to introduce myself to this doctor/deity. I told him my name and, before I could remind him of the letter, he hugged me. He remembered my letter. (How cute was that letter?) He remembered my name. We spoke. I told him I wanted to be a cardiologist. Then, for that someday when I would need a med school recommendation, DeBakey gave me his home phone number.

Today, you would have a better chance of getting Dick Cheney's cell phone number than your dermatologist's home number. Still, I never wound up making the call.

As a college sophomore, I told my parents I wanted to go into journalism, not medicine. It felt like I was copping to an unsolved murder. DeBakey's name didn't come up in my family for a long time.

Then, in the late eighties, when the world knew that doctors were fallible, drowning in the cost of malpractice insurance and often not even professionally happy, my father had an aortic aneurysm. By the dumb luck of a perfectly timed standard physical, a bubble was found in his aorta, maybe weeks shy of catastrophically bursting. The area had to be removed and replaced with a ring of Dacron.

During the five-hour operation, I told my mother, "Daddy's surgery was pioneered by ... DeBakey." My mother smiled wanly and looked around the hospital. "You know, I'm so glad you didn't become a doctor," she said.

DeBakey's procedure bought my father twenty years. He and my mather died within eight months of each other. For me, the loss of DeBakey felt like the last cut of all ties to the road not taken.

GET OUT IN FRONT
OF THAT EPITAPH

■ ■

ONCE WHILE DRIVING WITH THE heater on, top down, lights on and wearing sunglasses all at the same time, I realized that humans don't live forever. To this day, I haven't done anything about it. Other people have.

Suddenly, inanimate objects everywhere have plaques stuck to them: *This state-of-the-art electrified fence was donated to the children of Brentwood by Adolfo Frumington IV.* Sidewalks, hydrants, flagpoles—even trees—are turned into memorials, not to the deceased but to people currently enrolled in the human race.

This phenomenon is generational. Baby boomers, the increasingly ignored demographic, are getting the jump on death by self-memorialization. Not that the concept is new. Ramses II, who reigned over ancient Egypt for longer than the life expectancy of a modern Egyptian, was Donald Trump BC. We're the first, however, to memorialize the eternally anonymous.

A bench in Westwood branded a "Gift of Svetlana Platt Ruiz" may outlive its benefactor by centuries. What's Svetlana saying through her faux-cedar largesse? "My life has meaning" is what she's saying. Not only will that bench recall Svetlana as a patron of plump Americans in perpetuity, she can savor her legacy now, while her biological clock still ticks.

Really, you have to feel for people who died before we discovered our pre-death necrophiliac passion for ourselves. They may have had a stairwell posthumously named after them, but in life, they never got to say, "I have a stairwell named after me." Funny, it used to be enough of a legacy to have children. Not anymore.

As the kids grow up, we bifocus on them outside Jamba Juice, lost in their dreary teenage thoughts, and we fear that they're not fit to oversee our claim to having been significant two-legged mammals. But an engraved lifeguard stand won't quit school and marry our worst nightmare.

(Actually, I'm okay with this devaluation of children. People now grafting their names on sycamores once sang the praises of parenthood. As a childless man, I'd feel so left out. But now that the discussion has turned to self-edification/aggrandizement/adulation, I can jump right in.)

A big question is why it took so long for boomers to think of this. The probable answer: Some of us are dying. I read the obits today, oh boy. Or we get that phone call: Forty-two years old. Tennis. Dropped dead.

We whisper: Was there a family history of massive coronaries? If the answer is yes, we're relieved. Thank God, death ran in his family.

If it's no, we take our panic to our doctors. They could have coin-operated MRIs and a tip jar and we wouldn't care as long as they send us home strong. Honey, I have a head cold, but I'm gonna beat this thing. And when I do, I'm donating a pitching cage to the Little League with a 14-karat—no, 18-karat—gold-plated plaque above home plate.

Okay. Let's gauge where this trend stands in terms of overall pitifulness. On a scale of one to ten—one being Betty Ford, ten being Michael Milken—this is about a seven: behind using your name to promote addiction treatment but solidly ahead of pushing junk bonds before naming half of Santa Monica after yourself.

Then again, you don't want to leave it to someone else to interpret your legacy. Take Rosa Parks. Los Angeles named a strip of the Santa Monica Freeway the Rosa Parks Freeway. It's just a couple of miles from a sign dedicated to Christopher Columbus, who enslaved the kind of downtrodden people Rosa Parks had the guts to help liberate. But self-memorializing isn't about gaining perspective anyway. After all, people now name stars after themselves: That dot between Hydra and Canis Minor? That's Peter Mehlman.

MANDELA WAS LATE

■ ■

FRANKLY, AS A PAROLE OFFICER, you root for your thugs to come late or, better yet, not show at all. They get kicked back into the can where they belong, and you have time for a sandwich. But somehow, I felt different about Nelson Mandela. Maybe I was losing my edge, but he seemed somehow more respectable than most of the ex-cons who pollute my schedule.

In twelve-plus years, the only time Mandela missed a meeting was when he got a Medal of Freedom or some shit from some panel of European gasbags. Personally, I don't think getting sprung from the joint should get you any medals, but Mandela gave me eight months' notice and politely asked if we could reschedule. Thinking the bogus award might give him some positive reinforcement, I let him slide.

Clearly, I set a bad precedent, because now it was 11:03 a.m. and he was AWOL for his last meeting. I considered Mandela among the top fifteen most effective rehab jobs I'd ever done, but let's face it, you can't argue with statistics. The recidivism rate for a guy who does twenty-seven years in the clink is up there with the chances of your Beemer getting jacked in Johannesburg.

Jacking Beemers. If that's what Mandela's up to, I swear I'll run that self-destructive son of a—

My door swung open. It was Mandela. It took every muscle in my neck to keep from looking at my watch. Instead, I went through my routine, taking in his overall mien: blue blazer, white shirt, plum tie, gray "ANC Athletic Dept" sweatpants. Right off, the flashiness of the tie queered me. Maybe his ex-wife was back in the picture. What was her name?

I peeked at the file on my desk labeled MANDELA, NELSON (GUERRILLA/#20742-0019) and saw her name: Winnie. Right. My old colleague Briscoe was her parole officer. One day he went out on his lunch break to get his negative HIV results framed and was found with a pickax in his head.

Phrases like "material breach" and "consorting with known criminals" flooded my head. I stepped toward Mandela and frisked him: hankie, debit card, two-way pager, signed photo of Gwen Stefani, and the keys to every city on earth that has a mayor. I moved on. Subtly, I smelled his breath. A hint of scrambled egg whites, but nothing to raise any red flags. Mandela was clean. Still, my antenna was up. Way up.

"Have a seat, Nellie."

He lowered himself into a chair slowly, like Gandhi ten days into one of his crash diets.

"Rough night? You seem a little stiff."

"I'm eighty-four years old," said Mandela.

Of course. Every hood walking through my door thinks he's the victim.

"What have you been up to?"

"Today?"

"Today, yesterday, Tuesday. Whatever. Start with today."

"I had scrambled egg whites with Kofi Annan, a conference call with Colin Powell and posed for Richard Avedon."

Annan, Powell, Avedon. I made a note to run the names.

"But are you keeping busy?"

Mandela rolled his eyes. Oh, great, I thought. Here we go.

"Well, the press picked up on a talk I gave in which I referred to George W. Bush as 'a president who has no foresight, who cannot think properly'."

I bolted up. "I knew it! The same crap that got you in trouble last time."

"Yes," he said with cool defiance, "but now we live in a free country."

"Not for repeat offenders, it's not!"

Mandela threw me a facial expression I couldn't have read with an X-ray machine. Truth is, I'd forgotten about the whole "free country" thing. It took me twenty-five years to learn that the h in apartheid was silent, and by then the game was over. Mandela was right. Legally, I had no beef with him. That's my problem with cons like Mandela: they make me feel really unintelligent.

For ten seconds, Mandela and I didn't say a word. Luckily, I had time: My noon appointment had to cancel after he was shot to death on his way to picking up a new bulletproof Mercedes. Suddenly, I realized that irony was everywhere, and this whole charade was just a charade. Maybe Mandela would go straight, or maybe he'd backslide into the sludge of human rights. The fact is, people do what they do, whereas fish are driven mainly by instinct.

I cleared my throat and broke the silence.

"Hey, that Hugh Masekela can really blow the crap out of a horn, huh?"

I caught him off guard with that one. Mandela's face softened. He looked like he wanted to smile or become violently ill. Or maybe he'd split the difference and become nonviolently ill.

"Look, Nelson, we're done together. I'm ending your parole. You're free."

Mandela looked up joyfully and said, "Good. I was going to make some calls and have you fired anyway."

"Well, then, we've found some *common ground*, as you would put it."

At that, Nelson Mandela stood up, walked out, and I never saw him again.

But then, it's only been three weeks.

■ ACKNOWLEDGEMENTS ■

THE MAJOR THANKS GO JAMES and Rose Mehlman for passing on a sense of humor and a love of words. Their support for an unlikely career path was above and beyond anything imaginable, especially for two people raised in the Great Depression. James, gone five years now, used to ask, "Where did all this creativity come from?" I'd say, "From you," and he'd say, "Good answer." But it wasn't a good answer, just the truth.

More major thanks go to my brother, Jeff Mehlman, without whom I'd know little about thinking visually, dramatic structure, sneaking into Madison Square Garden, the greatness of Martin Scorsese, the Allman Brothers, Walt Frazier, Orson Welles and—especially—basketball, the coolest game on Earth.

Some very honorable mentions to endlessly funny, fascinating and inspiring friends: Bill Masters and Gail Berman, Mike Sager, Barry and Melanie Landsberg, Barry Wendroff, Robert Gibbs, Jaci Judelson, Karen Hermelin, David Mandel, A. J. Langer, Jennifer Grey, Stephen Glass, Deirdre Dolan, Chi and Landon Bui, Jared and Julia Drake, Diane Farr, Arthur Ashe, Jill Franklyn, Albhy and Melanie Galuten, Daryn Eller and Andy Alper, Terra Harper, Joeanna Sayler, Jeffrey Katzenberg, Bruce and Amy Karpas, Faith Kates, David Hume Kennerly, Suzanne Lanza, Jeff Ross, Michael Shedler, Jon Hayman, Stephanie Kennedy and Samson, Sharon Waxman, Katherine Blackmon, Tony Kornheiser, Pete Bonventre, Pete Vecsey, Morris Dees, Shannon Ensley and some others who'll come to mind when it's way too late, but hopefully they know who they are.

And finally, thanks to those who don't know who they are: John Updike, Philip Roth and Woody Allen.

■ PERMISSIONS ■

THE FOLLOWING PIECES WERE PUBLISHED in the same or slightly different form in the *Los Angeles Times*, "So Then They Gave Out the Emmy for Sitcom Writing and, Well, Yada, Yada, Yada..." (September 27, 1997); "Six Hundred Words For The Chatterers" (May 24, 2005); "L.A.: The Hedge-A-Dream Factory" (April 24, 2011); "An L.A. Story"(October 27, 2006); "Get Out in Front of That Epitaph" (August 28, 2005); "DeBakey's Heart" (July 16, 2008); "Okay, I'm Guilty; I Dodged Jury Duty" (November 28, 2009).

The following piece was published in the same or slightly different form in *Los Angeles* magazine "Moving Violations" (February 2002).

The following piece was published in the same or slightly different form in the *New York Observer*. "The Middle of Somewhere: Why I Hate To Travel" (November 10, 2008).

The following pieces were published in the same or slightly different form in the *New York Times*: "Star Trekking" (October 16, 1988); "Dear Guilty Mogul: Cough Up (September 28, 2003); "Dodging Potholes Along Memory Lane" (September 2, 2007); "Zuckerman Juiced" (November 14, 2005).

The following pieces were published in the same or slightly different form in *Esquire*: "Anxiety is Funny, Panic Is Hard" (February 2002); "Mandela Was Late" (August 2003).

The following piece was published in the same or slightly different form in *Entertainment Weekly*: "Notes From the Sitcom's Deathbed" (December 10, 2004).

Permissions

The following pieces were published in the same or slightly different form in *Huffington Post*: "Cold Case,O.J. Simpson" (November 20, 2006); "Numerology" (June 23, 2009).

The following piece was published in the same or slightly different form in *TheWrap*: "The Interchange" (May 14, 2012).

The following piece was published in the same or slightly different form in *SmokeLong Quarterly*: "Blank" (September 15, 2006).

■ ABOUT THE AUTHOR ■

PETER MEHLMAN, AFTER WHOM A hypochondriacal giraffe was named in the Madagascar movies, lives in in Los Angeles where he writes essays, screenplays, NPR commentaries and hosts the Webby-nominated YouTube series *Narrow World of Sports*. He grew up in Queens, New York, and graduated from the University of Maryland before writing for the *Washington Post* and ABC's *SportsBeat* with Howard Cosell. He has written for *Esquire, GQ, The New York Times Magazine* and virtually every Conde Nast women's magazine because of his powerful grasp on what women want. He was also a writer and co-executive producer of *Seinfeld*.

■ ABOUT THE PUBLISHER ■

THE SAGER GROUP WAS FOUNDED in 1984. In 2012 it was chartered as a multimedia artists' and writers' consortium, with the intent of empowering those who make art—an umbrella beneath which artists can pursue, and profit from, their craft directly, without gatekeepers. TSG publishes e-books; manages musical acts and produces live shows; ministers to artists and provides modest grants; and produces documentary, feature and web-based films. By harnessing the means of production, The Sager Group helps artists help themselves, *artifex te adiuva*. For more information, please see http://www.TheSagerGroup.net.

Printed in Great Britain
by Amazon.co.uk, Ltd.,
Marston Gate.